# DALLAS STARS

## `99
## NHL CHAMPS

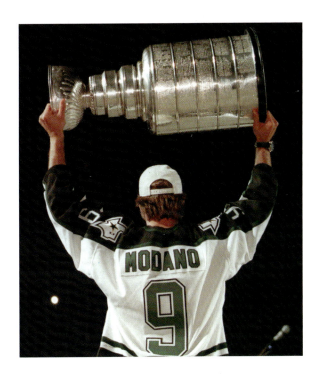

From the archives of

## The Dallas Morning News

Publishing by Sports Publishing Inc.
www.SportsPublishingInc.com

# The Dallas Morning News

**Burl Osborne,** Publisher    **Robert W. Mong Jr.,** President and General Manager
**Gilbert Bailon,** Vice President, Executive Editor    **Stuart Wilk,** Managing Editor

---

The Dallas Stars have brought hockey's prized Stanley Cup to the Sun Belt for the first time, thanks to their thrilling six-game triumph over the Buffalo Sabres in the 1998-99 Stanley Cup Finals.

The Dallas Morning News provided unequaled coverage of the Stars' journey, from the beginning of training camp in Vail, Colorado to the skate around the rink with the Cup at Buffalo's Marine Midland Arena. Bringing these events to the pages of The News required hard work and dedication on the part of numerous reporters, columnists, editors, photographers and administrators at the newspaper. Among those who were instrumental in assisting us in this project were Dave Smith, Deputy Managing Editor & Executive Sports Editor, Bob Yates, Sports Editor, John Davidson, Assistant Managing Editor, Visuals, Rick Choate, Anne Farrar, Martha Jansen, Jeff Miller, Paula Nelson, Guy Reynolds and William Snyder. From The News sports copy desk and photo staff, we specifically want to acknowledge the contributions of Gary Barber, Brian Bearden, Terry Bigham, Dawn Burkes, Jeff Cavallin, Susan Chalifoux, Kip Coons, Todd Davis, Jason Dugger, Jon Ehret, Carl Ellis, Dan Galvis, Dan Garcia, Javier Gonzalez, Kevin Gray, Dennis Hall, Joe Jansen, Mark Johnson, Ed Knocke, Mike Kondracki, Roxanna Pellin, Dave Renbarger, Jim Schnetz, Chuck Stewart, J.D. Talasek, Barry Vigoda, Laura Wade, Steve Waggoner, Vic West and John Zak. Also thanks to Jeff Cogen, the Vice President of Marketing and Promotion for the Dallas Stars.

*The Dallas Morning News*

## SPORTS PUBLISHING INC.

**Jennifer L. Polson,** Project Manager, Book Layout

**Terry N. Hayden,** Book Design

**Scot Muncaster,** Cover Design

**Joanna L. Wright,** Developmental Editor

**Susan M. McKinney,** Director of Production

@1999 The Dallas Morning News
All rights reserved. The reprinted articles and photographs were originally published in The Dallas Morning News. In some instances, articles appearing in this book have been edited to accommodate certain space limitations. However, whenever possible, we have included the articles in their entirety. All photographs are provided by News photographers Michael Ainsworth, Gary Barber, Louis DeLuca, Jon Freilich, Randy Eli Grothe, Michael Mulvey, Huy Nguyen, John F. Rhodes, Erich Schlegel, Andy Scott, Joe Stefanchik and David Woo.

Paperback: ISBN 1-58261-193-9
Library of Congress Number: 99-64794

Published by Sports Publishing Inc.
www.SportsPublishingInc.com

Printed in the United States

# CONTENTS

**1-31** Regular Season Playoff

**32-43** Playoff Rounds 1 & 2

**44-61** Western Conference Finals

**62-90** Stanley Cup Finals

# FOREWORD

The first time we met with our team before we went to Vail, Colorado, for training camp, general manager Bob Gainey stood up and said, "Our goal this year is to be a championship team. Our goal is to act and behave and play like champions."

After Bob talked, I stood up and said I wanted our group to be the tightest team, on and off the ice, that we can be. I said I wanted us to be prepared to make every sacrifice on a daily basis to win. Whether we would win any trophies and championships would be irrelevant unless we became a team.

We started putting a mindset into our team that if we stayed tight on the ice, and we stayed tight off the ice, then we could force other teams to crack. And that was our goal. Whether it was with our discipline, our work ethic, our positional play, our emotions, if we stayed at a high level, we could make people crack.

We felt it was important to develop an attitude within our group—a chemistry, a feeling—that we could accomplish a great deal by being together.

I put a lot of responsibility on our leaders, in particular, the captains, and relied on older players for advice.

Along the way, there was a shift in responsibility from the coaching staff to the leaders to the group. And the trust factor, as we moved along in the season, got stronger and stronger. It was really interesting to watch, not only our group coming together, but the players taking control of their destiny.

As the season moved on, the more control they took, the better we played. It was the players who were stoking the boilers and pushing themselves to a very high level. And the coaches were kind of painting the landscape as it moved on.

There was a bond of trust that developed between coaches and players. They listened, and they took it to heart. And they pushed themselves until the end harder than I ever could have pushed them.

The thing I'm proudest about the team is that they never lost sight of being a championship team. They knew as long as they stuck together and held tight, that they could win every night.

We're all proud that we won the Stanley Cup. We acted as one, and we stayed together through some very tough times. We never cracked.

You learn a lot about yourself and the group through an experience like this. The lesson we learned was that, no matter what your talent level is, by being able to stick together as tight as we were, you can accomplish a lot.

I think we proved that.

*—Stars coach Ken Hitchcock, June 22, 1999*

Brett Hull leaves the Reunion Arena stage following the post-parade rally on June 21.
(Louis DeLuca, The Dallas Morning News)

**DALLAS 4, BUFFALO 1**

October 11, 1998
Bill Nichols

# STARS DOMINATE BUFFALO, 4-1

*Power play whips Hasek in opener*

**The Stars can only hope that Saturday's opener is indicative of the season ahead.**

Their offense looked sharp against the game's best goaltender. They got goals from the players they need goals from while scoring on three power plays. And their defense, led by goaltender Ed Belfour, did the rest in a 4-1 victory over Buffalo before a sellout crowd of 16,928 at Reunion Arena.

Except for a lapse midway through, when they briefly let the Sabres back into the game, the Stars looked surprisingly polished.

"The way we moved the puck in the first 12 minutes, I haven't seen our team play like that," Stars coach Ken Hitchcock said. "There was some good transition to our game. But when we got up, 3-0, we played very casually with the puck, and that created momentum for Buffalo."

But by letting the Sabres back into the game, 3-1, at 15:22 of the second period, the Stars showed they can close the deal, too.

They killed four penalties in the final period, ending any hope the Sabres had of pulling even.

Ed Belfour (left) and coach Ken Hitchcock chat during the Stars' skate at the Dr. Pepper StarCenter in Irving, Texas. (John F. Rhodes, The Dallas Morning News)

Coach Ken Hitchcock voices his displeasure to the officials. (Dallas Morning News staff photographer)

Hey, who lost their bucket? A Stars helmet lays on the Reunion Arena ice. (Huy Nguyen, The Dallas Morning News)

These were important developments for the Stars, who were without Joe Nieuwendyk (knee), and Brian Skrudland (knee), and were playing defenseman Darryl Sydor and forward Jamie Langenbrunner, who were limited in their preparation because of contract holdouts.

Sydor opened the scoring as the Stars put Sabres goaltender Dominik Hasek on the defensive with three unanswered goals in the first period and a half. And Langenbrunner, with just four practices under his belt, set up the third one.

Dallas' other goals came from Mike Modano, who also had two assists, and Jere Lehtinen at the 19:16 mark of the third.

Eight power plays. Three goals.

"It was nice to get the power play off to a good start and get everybody involved and have different players score," Modano said. "The power play is going to be an important part of our game this season. Some nights you're going to have eight, nine, 10 chances on the power play."

Before the game, the Stars unveiled their Presidents' Trophy banner from last season, along with banners saluting their Central Division title and their Western Conference regular-season title.

"We were pretty excited," Pat Verbeek said. "When you've got a soldout crowd, it's good for at least one goal extra. We had a lull, but we took back control of the game. I think this shows that if we keep things simple, we'll have a chance to do well."

Although Hasek was strong early, holding off a flurry of Dallas shots, the Stars took advantage of Buffalo penalties to take control.

On Dallas' first power play, Modano flicked a quick pass across to Sydor, who sent his wrist shot over Hasek's outstretched glove. Modano then snuck in to steal one from Hasek just before the period ended, taking the puck off Hasek's pad and slipping it behind him at 19:09.

Then, on a three-on-one, Langenbrunner fed Grant Marshall in front. Although Hasek stopped Marshall's shot, Verbeek fought inside for the rebound, which he backhanded over the fallen Hasek. The Sabres, with 15 shots to Dallas' 11 in the second period, broke Belfour's shutout at 15:22 when Geoff Sanderson tipped in Alexei Zhitnik's slap shot on the power play.

"I really thought Langenbrunner's line played as a force," Hitchcock said of Langenbrunner, Verbeek, and Dave Reid. "As a group, our six defensemen played very well, and Eddie was strong to the end."

**DALLAS 3, DETROIT 2**

November 1, 1998
Bill Nichols

# HULL OF A DIFFERENCE

*Winger's two goals help Stars break Detroit's stronghold, 3-2*

**The Stars signed Brett Hull because they felt he might add the final ingredient needed to unseat rival Detroit and win the Stanley Cup.**

Hull supplied proof on Saturday night. His two goals made the difference in Dallas' 3-2 victory over the Red Wings before a sellout crowd of 16,928 at Reunion Arena.

After igniting the Stars with a goal just before the first period ended, Hull added the finishing touch to the comeback with a powerful slap shot from the circle that beat Detroit goalie Chris Osgood at 14:00 of the third.

Hull's one-timer off a no-look backhand pass from Mike Modano capped a furious contest between the NHL's best teams that lived up to its billing. The Stars' victory was not secure until the shot of Detroit's Nicklas Lidstrom banged off the post with 15 seconds left.

Stars coach Ken Hitchcock didn't need a fiery speech to motivate his players. They were playing the team that beat them in last season's Western Conference finals.

Brett Hull enjoyed great success against the Red Wings in 1998-99. (Dallas Morning News staff photographer)

Star goalie Ed Belfour followed up his October 31st victory against the Red Wings with a 5-1 triumph in Detroit on November 13th. (Dallas Morning News staff photographer)

"This was a game when you didn't have to say much as a coach," Hitchcock said. "You knew the game was on the ice. We had some ideas on matchups going into the game. But about 1 1/2 minutes into it, we sort of cashed those in. We just looked at our players and played who we thought was going well."

After Hull deflected Jere Lehtinen's shot past Osgood at 18:32 of the first period, the Stars scored 22 seconds into the second on Lehtinen's short-handed goal.

On the game-winner, Modano could hear the wide-open Hull shouting for the puck as Modano tried to negotiate his way through Detroit's zone.

"His voice is very noticeable on the ice," said Modano, who assisted on the tying goal and the game-winner. "It [the puck] just happened to be in the right spot when he got it off. Brett's a big-game player."

Hull, who had only two goals in the first eight games, wound up high on the one-timer, which snuck between Osgood's pad and the post.

"That doesn't happen anymore the way the game is played," Hull said. "A few years ago, you'd get that open every shift. There's not a lot of scoring right now. It doesn't matter who you are. To score 50 goals today, you've got to bury all of them."

> "That doesn't happen anymore the way the game is played. A few years ago, you'd get that open every shift. There's not a lot of scoring right now. It doesn't matter who you are. To score 50 goals today, you've got to bury all of them."
>
> — Brett Hull

The game also was a reversal for Dallas goaltender Ed Belfour, who lost his composure against the Red Wings in the playoffs.

This time, Belfour stayed composed, stopping the final 22 shots, several from point-blank range. And it was Osgood who lost his composure, hanging on to Pat Verbeek's stick, then getting into a shoving match with Verbeek that started a free-for-all at 18:07 of the third.

"We played with a lot of intensity, a lot of emotion," Hitchcock said. "I thought this was a real character builder for our team."

The Stars looked tentative early as the Red Wings took control with their tight passing. Detroit's Kirk Maltby scored first, then Steve Yzerman sent a high shot past Belfour.

But the Stars shifted the momentum just before the first period ended. Lehtinen skated halfway around the face-off circle, then fired his shot when Modano drew a defender away. Hull snuck into the slot to make the deflection.

Hitchcock said Hull is still adjusting to the Stars' system and that his performance showed he's close to being the player they expected.

"It's just difficult for Brett," Hitchcock said. "He was skating tough. He was understanding the movement of the puck. Tonight it looked like a good fit."

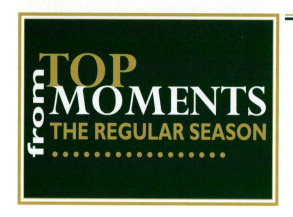

## from TOP MOMENTS
### THE REGULAR SEASON

**SAN JOSE 4, DALLAS 0**

November 5, 1998
Bill Nichols

# SHARKS CIRCLE HELPLESS STARS, 4-0

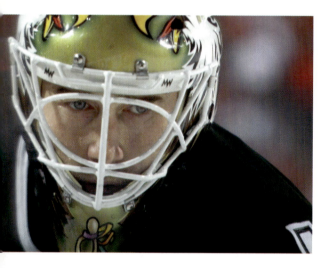

A dejected Ed Belflour. (Huy Nguyen, The Dallas Morning News)

### Belfour yanked; Dallas winless on road

**SAN JOSE, California**—The Stars, atop the NHL through their first nine games, fell hard in a 4-0 loss to San Jose on Wednesday night.

And the knockdown had nothing to do with Sharks tough guy Bryan Marchment, the player Dallas fans love to hate. Instead, the Sharks humiliated their fans' least favorite Star, goaltender Ed Belfour. Belfour has been booed in San Jose since he signed with Dallas after playing 13 games for the Sharks during the 1996-97 season despite San Jose offering him slightly more money.

But Belfour, who was booed each time he touched the puck, finally got a standing ovation from the crowd of 16,972 at the San Jose Arena

Dallas Star' left wing Jamie Langenbrunner (15) moves the puck ahead of San Jose Sharks' Mike Ricci, as teammate Joe Nieuwendyk follows, in the first period Wednesday, November 4, 1998, in San Jose, California. (AP/Photo/Ben Margot)

when he was replaced by Roman Turek at 10:04 of the second period.

Belfour allowed goals by Patrick Marleau, Ron Sutter early in the first period, then one to Jeff Friesen midway through the second.

So much for Dallas' five-game unbeaten streak. The Stars dropped to 6-2-2 while the Sharks (2-6-2) won only their second game of the season. The Stars, unbeaten in seven games at home, are 0-2-1 on the road.

The Stars, taking advantage of having only two road games in October, emerged from the first month with the NHL's best record at 6-1-2. But Dallas again showed its vulnerability on the road, looking much like it did in the other road games—a tie with Carolina and a loss to Chicago.

The Sharks quickly set the tone. On the first shift, San Jose winger Owen Nolan slammed Jere Lehtinen through the Sharks' bench door.

Then after Dallas' Brent Severyn was penalized for interference, Marleau blasted a slap shot between Belfour's stick and the far post just 3:30 into the game. Belfour was screened by defenseman Sergei Zubov.

Matteau's third goal of the season prompted a resounding chant of "Belfour, Belfour" from the fans.

Belfour didn't touch the Sharks' next shot, which came 39 seconds after the first goal. Sutter took a nice pass from Stephane Matteau in the slot, then fired a shot between Belfour's pads.

The Sharks had only three shots to the Stars' 10 in the first period, but they dominated. San Jose goalie Mike Vernon was strong. He saved two deflections by Brett Hull, then stopped slap shots by Zubov and Hull on Dallas' second power play.

Belfour, who entered the game with a 5-1-1 record and a 1.70 goals-against average, was way off his usual form. He was replaced by Turek after Friesen scored at 10:04 of the second. Friesen got in front of defenseman Darryl Sydor, then took Tony Granato's backhand pass and sent a wrist shot past Belfour.

Belfour received a standing ovation as he skated off.

Marchment, who was slapped twice in the face by Grant Marshall in the teams' first game on October 24 in Dallas, was relatively quiet.

Although he made a few good checks, he was on the receiving end of the hardest hit. Jamie Langenbrunner pinned Marchment to the boards just as San Jose was changing lines. With the bench door opened, Marchment hit the frame hard, and his helmet flew off. He walked straight past the bench and into the dressing room. But he returned moments later.

It was a disappointing performance for the Stars. They entered the game hoping to establish a road mentality after spending 17 days at home. In their only other road games, they blew leads in a tie with Carolina and a loss to Chicago.

"Our team is less concerned about San Jose and more concerned about being a really good road team," Stars coach Ken Hitchcock said before the game. "I think we're in first place right now because we've played more home games. What's really important is we have to learn to play for 60 minutes. You're not going to get points playing 40 minutes of hockey. On our last road trip, we played 40 minutes in both games."

The Stars better develop that mentality quickly. Four of their next five games are on the road.

> **"What's really important is we have to learn to play for 60 minutes. You're not going to get points playing 40 minutes of hockey. On our last road trip, we played 40 minutes in both games."**
>
> **—Stars coach Ken Hitchcock**

**DALLAS 5, DETROIT 1**

November 14, 1998
Bill Nichols

# STARS CRUSH WINGS

### Fired-up Dallas rolls to 5-1 win

DETROIT—Detroit players like to downplay their rivalry with the Stars. After all, the defending Stanley Cup champions say they have more important things to worry about during the regular season.

Captain Derian Hatcher runs over an unsuspecting Red Wings player. (Dallas Morning News staff photographer)

The Red Wings might want to get on board.

Friday's 5-1 victory was Dallas' second consecutive win over Detroit this season. And this domination took place at Joe Louis Arena, where the Stars were 1-17-2 the previous 20 games, including playoffs.

It seemed appropriate that the Stars ended the Joe Louis jinx. It was Friday the 13th, it was the Stars' 13th game of the season, and they were wearing their third jerseys for the 13th time.

"There was some fear on our side," Stars defenseman Craig Ludwig said. "We played on edge because we're sick of getting beat here."

While the Red Wings (8-7-0) might be waiting for the playoffs before getting excited about Dallas (8-3-2), the Stars played with desperation. After being shut out twice in the past three games, they were determined to initiate the action.

Joe Nieuwendyk breaks a Stars franchise record by scoring a break-away goal against Detroit's Chris Osgood just seven seconds into the game. (Dallas Morning News staff photographer)

It took seven seconds.

Joe Nieuwendyk, after losing the opening faceoff, stunned the Red Wings when he stole Uwe Krupp's cross-ice pass and took the breakaway in for a goal on Chris Osgood at 19:53. It was the fastest goal after the opening faceoff in franchise history, breaking Tony Hrkac's record of eight seconds set last Saturday.

That score also set the tone. The Stars forechecked relentlessly, played tough along the boards, and crowded in front of Osgood to score three more goals in the first period.

"That was big," Nieuwendyk said of his goal. "You get a quick goal and an early 4-0 lead here, it doesn't get much better than that."

Dan Keczmer's crunching hit on Detroit captain Steve Yzerman in the first period also had a big impact on the Red Wings. Keczmer slammed Yzerman, who lowered his head, into the glass. As Yzerman lay on the ice, Detroit's Darren McCarty tackled Keczmer from behind and drew a double minor for roughing.

On the power play, Darryl Sydor beat Osgood with a high slap shot for a 3-0 lead at 8:13. Yzerman left to get stitched up, but returned in the second period.

"It got their team pretty mad," Keczmer said. "I think it got both teams pretty motivated."

In the first period, Derian Hatcher knocked in a rebound and Grant Marshall snapped in a pass from Nieuwendyk as the Stars scored three times at even strength.

When the first period ended, the Red Wings left the ice to boos. And Osgood, who had the flu, was replaced by Kevin Hodson. Although Dallas had five penalties in the second period, Detroit's only score came on McCarty's tip-in on the power play. Mike Modano erased any hope of a Detroit comeback by stealing a breakout pass, beating Hodson to the puck, and flipping it over the fallen goalie.

"We've had some bad luck here for a long time, and the first period has been bad for us," Modano said. "That quick start was big. From then on, we took advantage of opportunities that we created. The excitement and enthusiasm was really back."

While this rivalry might be bigger from Dallas' perspective, the game might also have been more significant for the Stars. They corrected most of the flaws that have bothered them. They sustained a high level of energy, forechecked hard, rushed the net, and got four goals at even strength.

"We don't want to be just another notch on their gun belt," Stars coach Ken Hitchcock said of the Red Wings. "We wanted to give them something to think about."

> "We've had some bad luck here for a long time, and the first period has been bad for us. That quick start was big. From then on, we took advantage of opportunities that we created. The excitement and enthusiasm was really back."
>
> —Mike Modano

DALLAS 7, ST. LOUIS 3

December 16, 1998
Bill Nichols

# HULL, STARS GO ON OFFENSIVE

*Former Blue scores two goals to help Dallas rip St. Louis, 7-3*

**It was Brett Hull's kind of game.**

In his first contest against his former team, Hull scored two goals in an offensive outburst by the Stars that ended in a 7-3 victory over St. Louis before 16,928 at Reunion Arena on Tuesday.

It may have been Hull's first game back since missing seven of the last eight with a strained groin muscle. But he looked refreshed as he and the Stars greeted the Blues with a wide-open style.

Defense took a backseat to speed and transition in a high-octane pace that nudged fans to the edge of their seats and left Dallas with its most goals since scoring eight against Buffalo exactly one year ago.

Hull and Joe Nieuwendyk led the way, with two goals apiece, including Hull's breakaway that beat old friend Grant Fuhr.

"I like to score; that's what I do," Hull said. "It's not anything I was trying to do more of. They're a good club, and you have to score a lot to beat them."

Hull said he did not carry extra motivation in facing the team he spent more than 10 years with. He said hellos before and after the game,

Brett Hull reaches for the puck in first-period action vs. St. Louis. (AP Photo/L.M. Otero)

Craig Ludwig maneuvers past a Blues' player in action at Reunion Arena. (Dallas Morning News staff photographer)

including a conversation in the hallway with Fuhr in which Fuhr told him, "We'll do battle next time."

"I was really nervous before the game," Hull said. "I was just hoping it (the groin muscle) wasn't going to get tweaked again. After the first period, I felt good."

The Stars followed Hitchcock's pre-game advice by initiating the action. But while Hitchcock was looking for more of a physical initiation, he had no complaints after his players took it upon themselves to outskate the Blues at their own game. Complicating matters for the Blues was the absence of key players Pierre Turgeon and Geoff Courtnall, two of their top scorers.

In addition to Hull and Nieuwendyk, the Stars got goals from Grant Marshall, Pat Verbeek and Brian Skrudland as all four lines scored. That deep production handed the Blues a season high for goals allowed.

"It was, for us, a really different hockey game," Hitchcock said. "This was the most continuity we've had with our forwards. We played more open, but that wasn't by design. When you're playing against a team like St. Louis with speed, you want to skate with them."

Dallas regained the lead in the Western Conference, one point ahead of Phoenix with 39 points. The Stars (17-5-5) are unbeaten in their last six games (4-0-2). And Dallas, with a home record of 11-2-2, ranks first among NHL teams with 24 home points.

Hull played on the top line with Mike Modano and Jere Lehtinen, as Jamie Langenbrunner moved to the second with Nieuwendyk and Grant Marshall, and Mike Keane played with Verbeek and Tony Hrkac.

The teams combined for five goals in the first period. Dallas scored the first two as Marshall deflected in a pass from Derian Hatcher, and then Verbeek knocked in a rebound.

Verbeek's first even-strength goal this season capped a remarkable play. He passed to Tony Hrkac, who crossed the blueline, then dropped a pass in the high slot to Verbeek, who dropped a pass to Mike Keane. Jamie McLennan stopped Keane's shot, but Verbeek knocked the rebound into the open net.

After St. Louis scored two goals in a 34-second span, Hull scored his first goal on the power play with 42 seconds left in the period by deflecting Darryl Sydor's foot-high shot past McLennan. Goals by Skrudland and Nieuwendyk put Dallas in control. Then Hull's breakaway on Fuhr, who replaced McLennan after Nieuwendyk's goal, made it 6-3 with 2:04 left in the second.

> **"It was, for us, a really different hockey game. This was the most continuity we've had with our forwards. We played more open, but that wasn't by design. When you're playing against a team like St. Louis with speed, you want to skate with them."**
>
> **—Stars coach Ken Hitchcock**

DALLAS 0, COLORADO 3

February 8, 1999
Bill Nichols

# AVALANCHE FLATTENS STARS

*Belfour not up to task, 3-0*

**Sunday's Western Conference showdown between the Stars and streaking Colorado came down to goaltending.**

The Avalanche had it. The Stars did not.

Despite outshooting Colorado, 27-12, the Stars were shutout, 3-0, before 16,928 booing fans at Reunion Arena.

Patrick Roy's 46th career shutout extended the Avalanche's franchise-record winning streak to 12 games. It was his third shutout of the streak, putting the red-hot Avalanche (29-19-4) two points behind second-place Phoenix and six behind Dallas (30-10-8) in the Western Conference.

While the Stars owe much of their success to goalie Ed Belfour, he was not up to the challenge in this playoff-caliber contest. It was the second fewest shots Dallas has allowed this season.

"Our guys worked really hard, and I didn't play my best game," Belfour said. "It was definitely frustrating for myself and everybody else."

The Stars played with the tenacity they were hoping for. But Belfour surrendered a goal to Claude Lemieux on one of Colorado's two shots in the second period, one to Chris Drury in the third, then Jon Klemm's first goal of the season to put the game out of reach with 4:03 left.

Jamie Langenbrunner's shot on goal is stopped by Patrick Roy. (Dallas Morning News staff photographer)

The Stars' Derian Hatcher applies a big hit. (Louis DeLuca, The Dallas Morning News)

"To be blunt and honest, their goaltender outplayed our goaltender," Stars coach Ken Hitchcock said.

But Hitchcock didn't pin the loss on Belfour. He was also critical of his best players for not attacking the net and creating scoring opportunities by digging in the corners. The Stars suffered their fifth shutout despite having seven power plays.

"From a standpoint of play, I thought until the last two or three minutes, allowing that team less than 10 shots on goal was a great way to win that hockey game," he said. "I thought that offensively we weren't good enough, we weren't strong enough with the puck, and I don't think we were determined enough to go into those nasty areas."

The Stars had hoped to send a message to the Avalanche, which ended its four-game road trip with victories over Boston, Buffalo, Detroit and Dallas. The Stars came out with such high energy that they got several good scoring chances and sent two helmets flying from hard hits.

But the Avalanche never panicked despite its lack of shots. It played smart positionally, keeping the Stars out of the scoring lanes and letting Roy do the rest.

"They came out real strong in the first five minutes," Colorado coach Bob Hartley said. "It looked like a tornado out there. But we kept them to the outside and didn't give them many scoring chances."

The Stars could have had plenty. They rarely mustered shots from close range on their seven power plays. And Colorado's excellent penalty killing took some energy out of the Stars.

"You've got to make plays with the puck in a game like that," said Stars center Mike Modano, whose scoring streak was snapped at nine games. "Once we get the puck, we have to do something with it. It was a little bit of some parts of our game being bad and all parts of their game being good."

If this game was a measuring stick for the Stars, then they have some work to do to maintain their lead in the Western Conference. They are 5-3-2 in their past 10 games.

"Every game is a challenge, but you want to play a better game against a team that's hot," Belfour said. "I think our team played really well, and I didn't. That's when I need to come up with the big saves."

> "Every game is a challenge, but you want to play a better game against a team that's hot. I think our team played really well, and I didn't. That's when I need to come up with the big saves."
>
> —Ed Belfour

## TOP MOMENTS from THE REGULAR SEASON

DALLAS 4, NASHVILLE 3

February 24, 1999
Bill Nichols

# MODANO HAT TRICK LIFTS STARS

### Dallas rallies in 3rd, wins 4-3

**NASHVILLE, Tennessee**—Scrawled on the message board in the Stars' dressing room were the three keys to beating Nashville. No. 3 turned out to be the lucky number: "60-minute game."

That reminder served the Stars well as Mike Modano scored three goals for the second time in the past three games to lead Dallas to a 4-3 comeback victory over the Predators before 15,581 at Nashville Arena.

Modano's game-winning goal with four minutes, 23 seconds left in the third period capped the Stars' first comeback in 10 attempts this season when trailing after two periods (1-8-1).

Modano, who also got a hat trick on Friday against Chicago, posted his 300th career NHL goal with his seventh career three-goal performance.

Modano scored his 21st, 22nd and 23rd goals as Dallas unleashed a season-high 45 shots on goalie Mike Dunham in a lightning-paced game.

"Now I know how Brett feels," Modano said, looking over at linemate Brett Hull afterward. "I think I'm just getting in the right place at the right time, and the puck seems to be following me."

Mike Modano scored three goals against the Predators. (Dallas Morning News staff photographer)

Mike Modano received teammate's congratulations after a goal against Nashville. (Dallas Morning News staff photographer)

Dunham frustrated the Stars by holding on to a 3-1 lead despite the barrage of pucks. With the game slipping away, Pat Verbeek opened the floodgates with a goal at 7:50 of the third. Joe Nieuwendyk set up that score by taking the shot that Verbeek rebounded. It was Nieuwendyk's 800th career point.

"We were throwing everything but the kitchen sink at him, and we needed a break," Verbeek said. "That got us to within one, then Mo came up big."

Just 1:11 after Verbeek's goal, Modano stole the puck at Nashville's blue line, then raced in on Dunham. Modano gave him his favorite move, drawing the goalie to his left side of the net, then putting the puck on his forehand and cramming it between Dunham's sliding skate and the far post.

Then, at 15:37 of the third, Jere Lehtinen got control of the puck as he fought off Tom Fitzgerald behind the net, then slid a pass across the crease to Modano, who one-timed it past Dunham.

Asked if he said anything to the team during the second intermission, Modano said, "No, but Ken did," referring to coach Ken Hitchcock. "He had a lot to say. We just needed to come out strong and get that second goal. We knew if we let them get that fourth one, that would be trouble."

Although the Stars suffered some breakdowns to fall behind, their passion in the third period compensated. The win increased their lead over idle Phoenix in the Western Conference to 13 points. It also extended their unbeaten streak to seven games, their unbeaten streak in road games to eight.

"Holy smokes," Hitchcock said. "That was a revved up hockey game. You kind of want to burn the tapes of that one. It's a great win because we stayed with the program. We could have got discouraged, but our good players led the comeback."

Although the Stars scored first on Modano's one-timer off a centering pass from Hull in the corner, the Predators got goals by Blair Atcheynum and Scott Walker in the first period, and then Walker scored just 37 seconds into the second.

"We knew if we kept going it would change," Hull said. "We just stuck to our guns."

> "Holy smokes. That was a revved up hockey game. You kind of want to burn the tapes of that one. It's a great win because we stayed with the program. We could have got discouraged, but our good players led the comeback."
>
> **—Stars coach Ken Hitchcock**

DALLAS 4, ANAHEIM 0

March 13, 1999
Bill Nichols

## from TOP MOMENTS THE REGULAR SEASON

# BELFOUR BLANKS ANAHEIM

### 4-0 victory earns Stars playoff spot

**Before the Mighty Ducks of Anaheim got too carried away, the Stars gave them a reminder Friday night.**

The Ducks entered the game as one of the league's hottest teams, but left knowing the Stars are still the best. Dallas shut down high-flying wings Paul Kariya and Teemu Selanne and the NHL's best power play to snap Anaheim's unbeaten streak at eight games with a 4-0 victory before 16,928 at Reunion Arena.

With the victory, the Stars (42-12-10) became the first team to clinch a playoff spot. The win extended their lead over Colorado in the Western Conference to 18 points while improving their league-leading record at home to 23-6-4.

And for good measure, Dallas goalie Ed Belfour highlighted the fast-skating, physical game by landing a strong forearm shiver on Anaheim tough guy Jim McKenzie.

It was Belfour's fifth shutout of the season, 45th of his career, and the second game in which he's landed blows on an opponent. It was the

Joe Nieuwendyk tallied twice against the Mighty Ducks. (Dallas Morning News staff photographer)

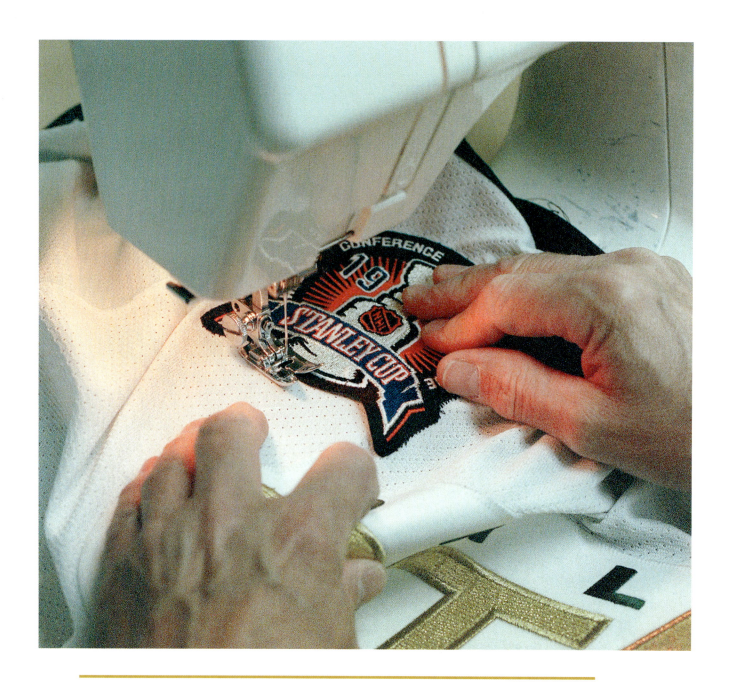

Though this patch wasn't sewn onto Stars' uniforms until weeks later, Dallas' victory over Anaheim clinched a playoffs spot. (John F. Rhodes, The Dallas Morning News)

fourth time Anaheim has been shut out and the first time since January 30 against Edmonton.

"I'm a competitor, and sometimes that happens," Belfour said of the right he landed on McKenzie, who took a run at the goalie behind the net, then cross checked him in front. "This was a real strong game for us, offensively and defensively. I was feeling good and seeing the puck well."

Just as important as Belfour's strong play was the Stars shutting down Selanne and Kariya.

Selanne, on a rampage with 15 goals and 14 assists in his past 17 games, had his point streak snapped just one short of the NHL's longest this season—18 by Philadelphia's Eric Lindros.

But Selanne and Kariya had nothing on Dallas centers Joe Nieuwendyk and Mike Modano. Tony Hrkac also scored for the Stars.

Nicole Bullack shows off her Stars tattoo at Reunion Arena. (Huy Nguyen, The Dallas Morning News)

Nieuwendyk, continuing his strong play, scored two goals to extend his point streak to nine games (8-6-14). It was his third straight multi-point game and his second straight two-goal game.

"I think we really respected this team," Nieuwendyk said. "We knew they had won seven in a row before Wednesday's tie with Vancouver. But people know it's not going to be an easy night when they play us."

As is usually the case when the Ducks play Dallas, Modano made a big impact, as did linemates Jere Lehtinen and Jamie Langenbrunner. They were primarily responsible for stopping Kariya, Selanne and Steve Rucchin.

Modano opened the scoring in the second period on Langenbrunner's wrap-around pass. Modano's 29th goal of the season was his 37th career point against the Mighty Ducks, the most of any player against them.

"As the game got on, we knew we had to stay patient," Modano said. "We've had a pretty decent track record against them. It's nice to shut down teams on a roll instead of people gunning at us."

The Ducks, with a 22.1 percent success rate on the power play, failed to score despite six attempts with a man advantage. They had one goal that was nullified because Fredrik Olausson's skate was in the crease when Selanne knocked the puck past Belfour midway through the third period.

"It didn't seem like a game that we lost by four goals," Selanne said. "I thought overall we played pretty well. We had a number of chances early, but we failed to bury them, and we had some errors that they capitalized on."

## from TOP MOMENTS THE REGULAR SEASON

DALLAS 5, ANAHEIM 1

April 8, 1999
Bill Nichols

# STARS POSITIVELY PRESIDENTIAL, 5-1

**It was fitting that the Stars clinched a share of their second straight Presidents' Trophy on a night when they ruled.**

In beating Anaheim, 5-1, on Wednesday, the Western Conference champions exerted their power (play) over the Mighty Ducks to assure themselves of finishing no worse than tied with Ottawa in the overall regular-season standings.

Although the Senators could still technically win a tiebreaker based on total wins, the Stars have five games to get one point and claim home-ice advantage for as long as they are in the Stanley Cup playoffs.

The Stars have 108 points. Ottawa, the Eastern Conference leader, lost to Toronto, 4-2, leaving it with 98 points with five games to play. The Senators would need to win out and have the Stars, who have not lost more than two straight all season, lose their remaining games.

Getting at least a share of the Presidents' Trophy is one of many achievements the Stars have wrapped up early. They clinched the Western Conference after beating Nashville, 3-0, on March 28.

Darien Hatcher (Dallas Morning News staff photographer)

The eventual Stanley Cup champion. (David Woo, The Dallas Morning News)

"The Presidents' Trophy means a lot to us," Stars center Guy Carbonneau said. "You have to take it as a compliment, but it doesn't give you the trophy you really want."

That would be the Stanley Cup.

But after going through some late-season struggles with injuries and a broken-down power play, the Stars showed against Anaheim how they can be a major contender for hockey's biggest prize.

They resurrected their power play, while virtually shutting down high-scoring wingers Teemu Selanne and Paul Kariya, who scored the Ducks' only goal. Dallas also got scoring from three of its four lines, received excellent goaltending from Ed Belfour and never let up with the lead.

And all that without injured players Mike Modano, Richard Matvichuk, Shawn Chambers and Brian Skrudland.

"Our focus is to build," coach Ken Hitchcock said. "We've got players coming back."

Hitchcock had a lot of strong players against the Ducks. Brett Hull scored twice, and Mike Keane, Pat Verbeek and Carbonneau scored the other goals. But there were others, such as defenseman Sergei Zubov, with three assists, and center Derek Plante, who had an assist and created several good scoring chances.

"We did the little things right," said Hull, who scored his 30th and 31st goals. "And that's what this team needs to do. We're not a bunch of fancy guys. We just played our game and were real solid defensively."

The Stars broke a four-game scoreless streak on the power play, which had not scored in its previous 14 attempts.

Although the Stars were only credited with scoring twice with the man advantage, they got a third goal just after Anaheim's Jeff Nielsen had stepped out of the penalty box.

"We showed our insistence with our forechecking and whack-and-hack," Verbeek said. "We got back to our tenacity on the power play. We kept things simple, and that's the key."

> **"The Presidents' Trophy means a lot to us. You have to take it as a compliment, but it doesn't give you the trophy you really want."**
>
> **—Stars center Guy Carbonneau**

**DALLAS 4, PHOENIX 2**

April 15, 1999
Bill Nichols

# STARS HAMMER COYOTES, 4-2

*Roenick leaves with broken jaw*

**Consider the message delivered.**

The Stars sent a strong one to rival Phoenix on Wednesday night in a board-rattling 4-2 victory at Reunion Arena that left blood on the ice and the Coyotes crying foul.

Dallas captain Derian Hatcher set the tone with a thunderous hit on Jeremy Roenick early in the first period.

Hatcher's crunching blow against the glass sent Roenick crumpling to the ice, his jaw broken in three places.

Hatcher received a five-minute major for boarding and an automatic game misconduct.

The incident will be reviewed by the NHL. Bryan Lewis, the league's director of officiating, attended the game and afterward made arrangements to have videotape sent to the NHL office.

While that hit ignited the Stars in a penalty-filled contest that had fans pounding the glass, the players downplayed any retribution for Roenick's hit on Mike Modano in the previous game in Phoenix. Roenick received a five-minute boarding penalty and a game misconduct after cutting

Craig Ludwig (3) and the Coyote's Dallas Drake battle against the boards. (Dallas Morning News staff photographer)

Dallas Stars' Derian Hatcher (2) is ejected during the first period after a hit that fractured the jaw of Phoenix Coyotes center Jeremy Roenick. (AP Photo/Eric Gay)

Modano's left eyelid on a hit away from the puck.

"I guess it's unfortunate that his jaw ended up being broken," Hatcher said. "His head was in a bad place. I got pushed from behind. I wanted to hit the guy, but I feel bad that he got hurt. It wouldn't have mattered who it was; I was going to hit him."

Afterward, in a profanity-laced tirade, Phoenix captain Keith Tkachuk attacked Hatcher for taking out the Coyotes' leading scorer, especially after "Hatcher said he was going to [expletive] hit him."

Stars coach Ken Hitchcock said he does not expect a suspension.

"Not at all," Hitchcock said. "The original call was two minutes, and because there was blood there, it went to five. It was a normal part of a game. The one thing that disappointed us was that Hatcher got pushed from behind from, I think it was Greg Adams. That's part of the game."

Phoenix general manager Bobby Smith said, "I have no [expletive] comment on that hit."

It was clear that the Stars sought payback in a series that could get uglier on Saturday in Phoenix. The past two games have been marred by the leading scorers of each team leaving with injuries. And the Coyotes and Stars could also meet in the second round of the playoffs.

While the Stars before the game had downplayed retribution over Roenick's hit on Modano, they spoke loudly after the puck was dropped.

As Roenick skated with the puck behind Dallas goal, Hatcher built up speed, then leapt as he smashed into Roenick. Hatcher's elbow caught Roenick in the face as they crashed into the glass.

"That same hit happens a lot," Hatcher said. "I didn't know it was him at first. Then we saw each other. We know how they play. They're a very physical team."

Roenick left the ice spitting blood, then stood in front of the Coyotes bench getting his loose teeth examined. He skated two more shifts before leaving the game. He will be evaluated Thursday.

The teams traded hard checks, slashes, high sticks and one fight. There were 12 penalties in the first period. The teams finished with 18 penalties—nine each—worth 53 minutes.

Modano scored first, when he backhanded a deflection of Brad Lukowich's shot past Mikhail Shtalenkov at 17:40 of the first. Just 1:09 later, Joe Nieuwendyk wristed a shot from the right circle that beat Shtalenkov on the far side.

In the second period, Sergei Zubov gave the Stars a 3-0 lead when he blasted a slap shot past Shtalenkov on the power play at 14:51.

The Coyotes broke Ed Belfour's shutout at 14:34 of the third, when Shane Doan knocked in Adams' pass in front. Phoenix then appeared to score just one minute later on Adams' shot from in front of the net, but the goal was nullified because the whistle had blown.

> "It was kind of playoff hockey. It was important to initiate and answer the bell because that's their game, to try to intimidate teams by banging them."
>
> —Stars forward Jamie Langenbrunner

But the Coyotes pulled to within one on Dallas Drake's rebound at 17:19. Phoenix had a good chance to tie when Nieuwendyk was penalized for tripping at 17:27. But the Stars didn't allow a shot on Belfour. Then Nieuwendyk's empty-net goal with 27 seconds left shut the door.

"It was kind of playoff hockey," Stars forward Jamie Langenbrunner said. "It was important to initiate and answer the bell because that's their game, to try to intimidate teams by banging them."

## PLAYOFFS ROUND 1
### VS. EDMONTON

**DALLAS 2, EDMONTON 1**

April 22, 1999
Keith Gave

# CAPTAIN NIEUWENDYK TAKES COMMAND, SPARKS STARS

Recently retired superstar Wayne Gretzky (left) returned to Edmonton for a ceremonial puck drop before play begins. Gretzky talks with the Stars' Joe Nieuwendyk. (Louis DeLuca, The Dallas Morning News)

**Safe to say no one among the Stars was looking forward to the start of the Stanley Cup playoffs more than Joe Nieuwendyk.**

Last spring the Stars enjoyed a wonderful six-week run through the post-season.

But the fun for Nieuwendyk lasted just two seconds short of 16 minutes.

That's when Bryan Marchment introduced himself by riding the Stars' leading goal scorer into the boards and wrecking a knee—Nieuwendyk's good one—exactly one year ago tonight.

"Some days you do fast forward in your mind to this particular moment," Nieuwendyk confessed a few hours before Wednesday night's

Dallas Stars Joe Nieuwendyk (25) and Darryl Sydor (5). (AP Photo/ David Duprey)

playoff opening 2-1 victory over Edmonton. "It was difficult watching last year, and it was a very difficult summer."

Nieuwendyk, who's wearing the captain's "C" in place of suspended defenseman Derian Hatcher, has had plenty of difficult summers since that joyous one in 1989, when he helped the Calgary Flames to the Stanley Cup. Since then, he hasn't played beyond the first round.

Twice in Calgary his Flames squandered 3-1 first-round series leads. Since coming to Dallas, he's had even worse luck. It was the shot off his stick into what he thought was a gaping net that Curtis Joseph gloved with a magical diving save. And we all know what Edmonton's Todd Marchant did just seconds later at the other end of the rink.

Last spring, Nieuwendyk started the playoffs as if he were riding shotgun on the space shuttle, scoring the opening goal of the playoffs at 2:22 and peppering goaltender Mike Vernon with four shots until the injury that put him on crutches. He picked up Wednesday where he left off prematurely a year ago.

With the Stars looking nervous and tentative at the start, Nieuwendyk was one of the few among them playing with any purpose. He had the series' first shot on goal 9:17 into the game, batting a bouncing puck into goaltender Tommy Salo's pads. Nieuwendyk had two of Dallas' three shots in the first period and four of its first six in the game.

You want leadership? Nieuwendyk provided it by example, fighting through heavy traffic against a team intent on finishing every check.

"He played fearless, which is good," coach Ken Hitchcock said. "He almost played reckless, which makes him a very dangerous player. And that's great for us."

After leading all Canadian-born goal scorers with 39 last season, Nieuwendyk started this season a month late while his knees mended following off-season surgery on both of them. And still he finished with 28 goals, including eight game-winners, among 55 points.

But it wasn't easy. Early in the season, his body had difficulty executing what his mind told him to do on gimpy legs. And his confidence wavered.

"The thing you run into if you're not careful is you start losing your focus," he said. "You come back and nothing happens for you. You start thinking, 'I'm not scoring. I'm not getting any chances. It's because of my knees.' So I just tried to simplify things and not worry about the scoring.

"I concentrated on the skating. As long as my skating was getting better, everything else followed. I learned that if you think about it too much, you can go crazy."

In the days and hours leading up to Wednesday's playoff opener, Nieuwendyk understood the importance of a long playoff run in a town whose hockey mantra has been Stanley Cup or bust for three straight springs.

"I think anything less than getting there this year will be a disappointment," he said, fully accepting the challenge. "This is what we all live for. . . .Everybody wants a shot."

Some guys just deserve it more than others. Nieuwendyk seems to be enjoying his.

> "He played fearless, which is good. He almost played reckless, which makes him a very dangerous player. And that's great for us."
>
> **Stars Coach Ken Hitchcock on Joe Nieuwendyk**

EDMONTON SERIES RE-CAP

June 22, 1999
Dan Noxon

# IT'S ALL STARS IN SERIES SWEEP

The record will show the Stars opened the 1999 Stanley Cup playoffs with a four-game sweep of Edmonton. That the teams played only four games is more of a technicality than anything, though. It's difficult to imagine four games that could have better prepared a team for a grueling post-season run.

Thanks to the sometimes brilliant goaltending of Edmonton's Tommy Salo, all four games were decided by only one goal, a trend that continued for Dallas throughout the post-season. The teams either were tied or the Oilers led in the third period of every game. The finale, in essence, was two games. Sergei Zubov's shot from the point bounced off Joe Nieuwendyk's leg and past Salo for the series-clinching goal at 17:34 of the third overtime, only 2 1/2 minutes shy of the equivalent of two games. It finished just after 2 a.m. Dallas time.

Linesman Kevin Collins (right) deftly gets out of the way as Edmonton's Roman Hamrlik fires the puck past Dallas' Shawn Chambers into the Stars' zone during Game 2 of the first round of the Stanley Cup playoffs. (Huy Nguyen, The Dallas Morning News)

Dallas' Joe Nieuwendyk (far left) fills the net and empties the building with the deflection that ends Game 4 at Edmonton. Nieuwendyk and Jamie Langenbrunner (far right) combined for all three Dallas goals in the six-period game that ended just after 2 a.m. Dallas time. (Louis DeLuca, The Dallas Morning News)

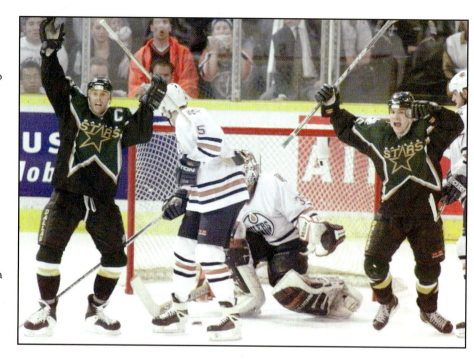

"This series is really going to help us down the line," Stars coach Ken Hitchcock said in the morning's wee hours following Game 4, "because we really had to push the envelope. Emotionally, physically, we just had to dig really deep."

The closeness of the games represented only part of the equation in preparing the Stars for a long and difficult run, though. The younger, faster—and sometimes bigger—Oilers entered the series with the attitude that they could pound the Stars into submission.

The hitting was ferocious, and Dallas had to play without Derian Hatcher, who had to watch his team's first five playoff games because of a league suspension. Hatcher received a seven-game suspension late in the regular season from National Hockey League commisioner Gary Bettman for his hit that broke the jaw of Phoenix star Jeremy Roenick.

The Oilers delivered a whopping 64 hits in Game 1. Included was Doug Weight bashing veteran center Guy Carbonneau from behind and into the boards. Weight received a game misconduct for the hit, Carbonneau a two-inch gash on his cheek that required stitches.

That wasn't good enough for Edmonton, though. The Oilers said they wanted to eclipse 100 hits in Game 2. They fell short but were credited with 65, not including rookie tough guy Georges Laraque's failed, flying attempt at Craig Ludwig's head that nearly brought down half the glass behind the Stars' goal.

"Just try to wear 'em down," said the Oilers' Todd Marchant. "The longer the series goes, the better chance we have."

While the Oilers kept hitting, Dallas kept losing players. Carbonneau was lost for the remainder of the series at the end of Game 2 with a sprained knee. Hatcher's defensive partner, Richard Matvichuk, went down with a groin injury midway through Game 3, as did forward Grant Marshall. Tony Hrkac sustained fractured ribs in Game 4 and didn't return until the Finals.

Plus, Pat Verbeek still was a week away from returning after injuring a knee late in the regular season.

But the Stars did what they had the previous two regular seasons while winning consecutive Presidents' Trophies as the league's top team—they simply overcame. They overcame the injuries. They overcame Edmonton's desire to take more shots at bodies than at goalie Ed Belfour. Most important, they overcame on the scoreboard.

En route to the Cup, the Stars would tie the NHL playoff record for six comebacks when trailing at any point during the third period, and they started immediately in the Edmonton series.

Jere Lehtinen scored 13 seconds into the third period to tie Game 1, and Carbonneau gave Dallas a 2-1 victory when he scored with less than six minutes remaining. The teams were tied again in the third period of Game 2 before Lehtinen and Jamie Langenbrunner scored four minutes apart, and then Dallas held off Edmonton's late charge.

The Oilers grabbed a 2-0 lead early in the third period of Game 3, but the unrelenting Stars rallied with goals from Mike Keane, Mike Modano and Nieuwendyk.

Then came Game 4—if you can call it just one game. Langenbrunner scored midway through the third period to tie the score, and it remained that way for quite a while. A first overtime passed with no scoring, then a second and very nearly a third in what was the longest game in Stars franchise history and the 12th-longest game in NHL history.

> "This series is really going to help us down the line, because we really had to push the envelope. Emotionally, physically, we just had to dig really deep."
>
> —Stars coach Ken Hitchcock, in the morning's wee hours following Game 4

The Stars received an eight-day break before resuming in the second round. In a way, the long layoff could have spelled trouble, because long layoffs in the post-season can stop momentum cold. But the team needed the rest, too. Every player agreed their opening series seemed more like a seven-game victory than a four-game sweep.

And that prepared them for even bigger challenges ahead.

### PLAYOFFS ROUND 2
### VS. ST. LOUIS

**DALLAS 2, ST. LOUIS 1**

May 18, 1999
Tim Cowlishaw

# MODANO REKINDLES MAGIC WITH HULL

Dallas' Brett Hull (right) gets reacquainted with former St. Louis teammate Grant Fuhr during the teams' second-round playoff series. (Michael Mulvey, The Dallas Morning News)

**ST. LOUIS**—Eventually, the Mike Modano-Brett Hull divorce was annulled. It had less staying power than a Dennis Rodman-Carmen Electra marriage.

It was just five days ago here that Ken Hitchcock broke up the two high-dollar forwards to try to get Modano going, to try to get Hull going, to try to get something going.

But just two games later, early in Monday's first period, they were back on the same line with Jere Lehtinen. Then, nearly three hours later, they were together again. The Stars might not have survived any other way.

Hull from around behind the net to Modano . . . and HE SCORES.

That's how it ended 2:21 into overtime at the Kiel Center on Monday. That's how it all ended in six games for St. Louis, a team that will go into the off-season convinced it was better than the Stars in four out of six games.

Dallas Stars Brett Hull (22) and Mike Modano. (AP Photo/Tim Sharp)

Brett Hull (tight) celebrates with Stars teammates Jamie Langenbrunner (center) and Darryl Sydor (Gary Barber, The Dallas Morning News)

History will say otherwise. The Stars advanced to the Western Conference finals after Modano scored his first NHL playoff overtime goal.

"It's really sweet when you win it on the road," said Modano. "You talk about working hard and trying to make the simple play, but it gets a little tense out there. Tonight Brett did all the grunt work on both goals."

"I had no idea we'd be back together tonight," Hull said. "That's something the coaches decide. They try to get a little bit of wealth and grit on each line."

No shortage of wealth on this line. Modano—$43.5 million for six years. Hull—$17 million for three. Only Lehtinen's still slugging along at under $2 million per year, but that, too, will change. And after Monday night, no one will convince Tom Hicks that he has spent unwisely on his star Stars.

Modano mentioned after Monday's game that it would be nice to get another crack at the Red Wings. But just getting a shot at someone was the goal, and three games into this series, Modano knew he wasn't contributing much to that effort.

The best forwards in the first three games were Joe Nieuwendyk and the Blues' Pierre Turgeon and Pavol Demitra. The best forward in the final three games? No question it was Modano.

Hitchcock's line shakeups were really designed to benefit Modano more than anyone. Putting Grant Marshall on his line gave him another grinder to get him the puck. It also sent the message that he needed to deliver some scoring.

Modano said the layoff between the first and second rounds had sucked the life out of his game.

"It was night and day from the first three games of this series to the last three," he said. "I was in that groove of playing every other day, and for some reason sitting out those seven or eight days just killed me."

Modano went to Stars general manager Bob Gainey for advice halfway through this series. It was a turning-point conversation.

"Bob has been around me for 10 years, and he knows my game better than anyone," Modano said. "A lot of burden was really weighing me down. The one thing Bob really told me was to try not to focus on the wins and the losses. "It's easier answering questions to the media, but it's harder to answer questions of teammates when you're disappointed."

No one is coming to Modano this week to ask why, to ask what happened. They are asking only whether he has a preference, Detroit or Colorado. It's a great question to be hearing this time of year.

"We're halfway there," Modano said, eyes on the prize. "It's been a month of great hockey. It gets tougher and tougher now. We all understand what's at stake here."

Modano senses the pressure. Regardless of the Hulls and Belfours that join this club over the years, Modano will remain the focal point, the brightest star of Stars.

It is his responsibility to see this team succeed, and, yes, that is a burden.

It didn't weigh him down Monday night as he turned the Blues loose for the summer and delivered the Stars one step closer to hockey in June.

ST. LOUIS SERIES RE-CAP

June 22, 1999
Ken Stephens

PLAYOFFS
ROUND 2
VS. ST. LOUIS

# STARS ELIMINATE BLUES IN SIX

**Hockey fans got more than their money's worth in the Stars' second-round playoff series against the St. Louis Blues.**

Instead of the usual 60 minutes of hockey, four of the six games extended into overtime.

The Stars opened the series with a 3-0 victory in Dallas. Pat Verbeek, who missed the Edmonton series with a knee injury, scored the opening goal and in other ways set the tone. Brett Hull victimized his former team for his first goal of the playoffs, and Mike Modano added the Stars' third goal. Meanwhile, Stars goalie Ed Belfour stopped all 23 shots on goal for his fifth career playoff shutout.

Late in the game, however, Verbeek gave St. Louis center Pierre Turgeon a wicked slash to the back of a knee. That earned Verbeek not only a penalty but also a one-game suspension.

Though the Stars were without Verbeek in Game 2, they finally got defenseman Derian Hatcher back after his seven-game suspension for the jaw-breaking hit on Phoenix's Jeremy Roenick late in the regular season.

Stars coach Ken Hitchcock surveys the action from behind the bench during Game 2 of the Western Conference semifinals at Reunion Arena. (Huy Nguyen, The Dallas Morning News)

No one's really very interested in the puck as St. Louis' Blair Atcheynum mixes it up with Dallas' Shawn Chambers and Darryl Sydor during a stoppage in play. (Huy Nguyen, The Dallas Morning News)

The Stars and Blues traded the lead four times in Game 2. The Blues led, 4-3, in the third period until Jere Lehtinen scored with 4:22 to go. At 8:22 of overtime, Joe Nieuwendyk wristed a sizzling shot past Blues goalie Grant Fuhr to give the Stars a 5-4 victory.

The series then shifted to St. Louis for another overtime thriller. Dallas led Game 3 early on a power-play goal by Hull, but St. Louis came back with scores by Mike Eastwood and Jochen Hecht heading into the third period. Darryl Sydor scored for Dallas to send the game into overtime, but St. Louis' Pavol Demitra scored 2:43 in to give the Blues' their first victory, 3-2.

The Stars and Blues went to overtime for the third consecutive time in Game 4, also played in St. Louis. Modano scored just 59 seconds into the game for Dallas. But the Blues answered with two goals in the second period, one of which deflected off Modano's stick. Lehtinen scored in the third period to again force overtime.

At 5:52 of OT, Stars defenseman Sergei Zubov, back in his own zone, tried a pass up the middle for Nieuwendyk instead of sending the puck off the boards. The Blues' Turgeon intercepted, then streaked in on Belfour, firing a high, stick-side shot for the 3-2 winner.

"We can't have that," Stars coach Ken Hitchcock said of Zubov's gaffe. "He knows it. We all know it. There was nothing there."

Back in Dallas for Game 5, Dallas regained the lead in the series with strong special-teams play.

During a penalty kill early in the first period, Modano stole the puck from Chris Pronger and carried it deep into the St. Louis zone before passing to Lehtinen, who one-timed it over Fuhr for a 1-0 lead. Dallas' power play, 1-for-20 through the first four games of the series, had a surge when Jamie Langenbrunner and Nieuwendyk scored with the man advantage. With a 3-0 lead in the second period, the Stars then went into a defensive shell and hung on for a 3-1 victory despite being outshot, 31-16, including 25-9 over the last two periods.

"They won the special-teams battle," St. Louis' Pronger bemoaned. "That's what cost us the game."

The Stars' Brett Hull gets a hug from teammate Brad Lukowich after Hull gives Dallas a 1-0 lead over his former team less than four minutes into Game 3 of the Western semifinals. It looked like Dallas was on its way to a 3-0 series lead, but the Blues rallied and won in overtime. (Huy Nguyen, The Dallas Morning News)

For Game 6, the Stars returned to St. Louis' Kiel Center, where they were 0-5-1 in their previous six games.

But Hull proved to be his old team's nemesis. He set up the tying and winning goals in a 2-1 overtime victory that sent the Stars on to the Western Conference finals.

St. Louis led, 1-0, until late in the third period, when Hull centered a pass to Derek Plante —who didn't even play in four of the Stars' previous nine playoffs games—for a goal that tied the score at the 13:58 mark. Then, 2:21 into overtime, Hull went into the corner for the puck, fought off the Blues' Craig Conroy and backhanded a pass in front to Modano. Modano sent a backhander at Fuhr, then forehanded the rebound between Fuhr's legs for the goal.

"I was walking off crying last year because I knew I wasn't going to be playing with the St. Louis Blues again," Hull said. "Now, I'm walking off here after beating that organization and going on in the playoffs."

# PLAYOFFS WESTERN CONFERENCE FINALS

**COLORADO 2, DALLAS 1**

May 23, 1999
Tim Cowlishaw

## ROY MORE FORMIDABLE THAN DETROIT

**For the first time in five years, the Western Conference finals are being conducted without any help from the Detroit Red Wings. That was good news for Dallas early Saturday evening.**

It was a lot better news for Colorado late.

The Red Wings weren't here Saturday, but Dallas finds itself in the same unenviable position it assumed at this time last year. Home-ice advantage is gone after just one game of the conference finals. Colorado's 2-1 victory ended the Stars' run of perfection at home in the playoffs.

A year ago, Detroit captured Game 1 at Reunion Arena. The home teams won the next five games, and the series was over. Detroit was on its way to another Stanley Cup.

Detroit's absence Saturday surely attributed to Colorado's only poor period, the first. Thrilled to be done with the Wings, the Avalanche saw Brian Skrudland on the ice and thought this was going to be the Florida Panthers all over again.

That's no knock on the former Florida captain who actually played quite well Saturday. But Colorado played a loose opening period before getting serious and proving to be the better team in the second and third.

Colorado rallied to score twice—well, three times if you own a Colorado driver's license, because in that case, you know that Valeri

Stars goalie Ed Belfour makes a kick save on this shot, but the Avalanche eventually prevailed, 2-1, in Game 1 of the Western Conference finals. (Huy Nguyen, The Dallas Morning News)

The Stars and Avalanche mix it up in front of the Dallas net. (The Dallas Morning News, Louis DeLuca)

Kamensky's second-period goal should not have been disallowed.

Still, for any locals who breathed a sigh of relief when the Avalanche eliminated the Red Wings, Saturday night served as a useful wake-up call. Be real. Colorado with a hot Patrick Roy is the worst assignment a team can get in the conference finals, certainly more dangerous than Detroit with a hobbled Chris Osgood in the nets.

Roy has produced a .957 save percentage in winning five straight playoff games. That qualifies as hot.

Roy also is the owner of three Stanley Cup rings. There is a reason for this. When he has played in the conference finals, his teams are 4-1, and the only tried and true formula for success against Roy is the one Detroit unveiled two years ago.

It's easier said than done, but you have to take goaltending out of the equation. Although Mike Vernon won the Conn Smythe Trophy two years ago (a questionable choice), the Red Wings as a team so badly outplayed Colorado, creating more chances and shutting down the Colorado power play that goaltending was all but irrelevant.

If the Stars are to regroup and advance beyond this round, it will be because they dominate play at both ends to the extent that the Roy vs. Ed Belfour storyline vanishes.

As long as the teams are evenly matched at all other spots, Dallas can't win. It's not so much due to deficiencies on Belfour's part, although he must one day win the Cup to silence his critics. But this is Roy's time of year. The Avalanche believes that, and the Stars are finding it hard to dispute.

"You start second-guessing yourself against Roy instead of just trying to get the puck on the net," said Stars center Mike Modano, who set up Dallas' only goal.

Roy made one mistake all night, wandering out of his crease and leaving the net wide open on Brett Hull's goal. But even that mistake would have meant nothing had Colorado defenseman Adam Foote not funneled the puck along the boards straight to Modano.

Roy stopped the next 25 shots and dominated the game.

> **"The one thing we have to get better at is not giving them easy odd-man rushes. They had a two-on-one and three three-on-twos, all caused by us not getting the puck on the net."**
>
> **—Stars coach Ken Hitchcock**

This loss will be a tough one for the Stars because they didn't make egregious mistakes they can talk of correcting. The power play was 0-for-2 but it wasn't the abomination it was for so much of the St. Louis series.

But now if the Stars truly have a deeper defense—and that may be in dispute as long as Shawn Chambers is out—they must prove it. If they really have stronger third and fourth lines, they must prove it. If their Presidents' Trophies mean anything more than Colorado's in 1997 (which was no help against Detroit), they must prove that, too.

The Stars won 55 percent of the faceoffs, which is just about the cutoff point for success. Anything less and you are letting Colorado, with superior skill people, play with the puck for too long.

"The one thing we have to get better at is not giving them easy odd-man rushes," Stars coach Ken Hitchcock said. "They had a two-on-one and three three-on-twos, all caused by us not getting the puck on the net."

The Stars don't have a sense of history with Colorado the way they do with Detroit. They had better create one fast if they don't wish to become history.

DALLAS 4, COLORADO 2

May 25, 1999
Bill Nichols

## PLAYOFFS WESTERN CONFERENCE FINALS

## FULL OF FIRE

*Relentless Stars pepper Avs' Roy with 45 shots*

Game 2 of the Western Conference finals looked a lot like Game 1. A key goal was disallowed, then the player who scored it contributed to the game-winner.

But this time, it was the Stars who stormed back from a controversial call to beat Colorado, 4-2, before 17,001 Monday night at Reunion Arena.

The Stars, who outshot Colorado, 45-19, tied the series, 1-1, with Game 3 in Denver on Wednesday. The loss left the Avalanche one game short of an NHL playoff record for road wins at seven.

"I think we just played desperate," Stars coach Ken Hitchcock said. "We knew if it went 0-2, we'd be in big trouble. We turned it into a street fight."

By employing a stronger physical base, the Stars dominated the flow of the game. They kept the pressure on goaltender Patrick Roy, shut down Colorado's top line, and allowed only one shot in the third period.

Yet, the Stars still needed dramatics to win. And there were plenty, including Joe Nieuwendyk's fourth game-winning goal of the playoffs at 11:52 of the third. With the score tied, 2-2, Dallas' Pat Verbeek appeared to score at 6:58 of the third. But after a review, officials ruled that Verbeek's skate entered the crease before the puck. It was a difficult call because the puck bounced off the skate of Verbeek, who was being pushed from behind by defenseman Jon Klemm. The puck went off

The Stars' Joe Nieuwendyk (25) takes the rebound of a shot by Pat Verbeek and pokes the puck beneath Colorado goalie Patrick Roy for the game-winning goal as Dallas knots the Western finals at one game each. This was Nieuwendyk's fourth game-winning goal of the playoffs. (Huy Nguyen, The Dallas Morning News)

No, he's not reading the label. Stars defenseman Richard Matvichuk (left) performs his pre-game ritual of repeating reminders into his helmet during the national anthem before Game 2 of the Western finals against Colorado at Reunion Arena. Teammates Brett Hull (center) and Mike Modano find their headgear less conversational. (Gary Barber, The Dallas Morning News)

Verbeek's skate again before he put his stick out as the puck crossed the goal line.

In Game 1, Valeri Kamensky had a goal disallowed, then came back to score the game-winner in the 2-1 victory.

"You know, Dallas, they're like us," Roy said. "They didn't let down. They kept coming at us. They threw everything they can at us."

Less than five minutes later, Verbeek sent a one-timer at Roy, then Nieuwendyk knocked the rebound through Roy's legs for the game-winner.

"The disallowed goal was disappointing, but I think everybody was pretty pumped the way we were playing, and we didn't let that get us down," Nieuwendyk said. "We wanted it a little more than they did."

Dallas outshot Colorado, 15-1, in the third period, and Mike Modano got the insurance goal with a wrist shot over Roy at 16:28.

The Stars played as though they were facing elimination. They checked with much more aggression than Game 1, and controlled the puck in Colorado's end.

"We didn't do a good enough job in their end the last game," Verbeek said. "When we're able to control the puck in the offensive zone, we generate a lot of scoring chances."

Hitchcock made a key change by putting Modano's line against Joe Sakic's line and Guy Carbonneau's line against Peter Forsberg's.

Carbonneau frustrated Forsberg, who had a goal and an assist in Game 1, with his aggressive play. Forsberg had one shot and one hit. Carbonneau had six hits. And Modano was the best skater on the ice.

"We just wanted to change our psyche a little bit," Hitchcock said. "We needed to turn the game into a different type of game—a little bit less free flow."

Despite Dallas' dominance, the Avalanche scored first when Sandis Ozolinsh knocked in a rebound at 10:32. But at 14:11 of the first, Dave Reid burst in on Roy from the goal line, then zipped a high wrist shot past Roy into the far corner.

Adam Foote (right) and Patrick Roy (left) sandwich a Stars player. (Gary Barber, The Dallas Morning News)

Sergei Zubov put the Stars ahead with a slap shot over Roy's right shoulder early in the second, but Milan Hejduk kept the Avalanche in the game when he put in a rebound at 14:59.

But the third period was all Dallas.

"I can answer the entire game with one answer: They had better legs than us, they were hungrier than us and they deserved the game," Colorado coach Bob Hartley said. "They played, and we didn't play."

## PLAYOFFS WESTERN CONFERENCE FINALS

**DALLAS 2, COLORADO 3**

May 29, 1999
Bill Nichols

# FIT TO BE TIED

***Rookie's overtime goal evens bruising series, 2-2***

**DENVER**—It took two shots for Colorado to climb back into the Western Conference finals. Then it took the rest of three periods and one overtime for the Avalanche to stay there.

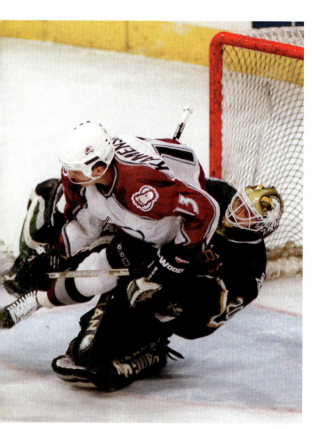

Valeri Kamensky plows into Stars goalie Ed Belfour in Game 4 action. (Dallas Morning News Staff Photographer)

After scoring on its first two shots of the game, the Avalanche held off the Stars in a 3-2 overtime victory Friday before 16,061 at McNichols Arena. Rookie Chris Drury took a pass from Sandis Ozolinsh and fired the game-winner past Ed Belfour, high on the stick side, with 31 seconds left in overtime. So the series returns to Reunion Arena for Game 5 on Sunday tied, 2-2.

"That's a tough way to lose," Stars coach Ken Hitchcock said. "When you've got a hockey game this hard, and this well played, I don't know how you can be unhappy. We've got two teams that are maxing out. There's nothing left in the gas tanks."

After losing two straight, including a 3-0 shutout at home in Game 3, the Avalanche could not afford another loss. Colorado scored on its first two shots in the opening 4:54, with Joe Sakic getting his first point of the series, then Shjon Podein scoring the other.

But the Stars patiently came back, scoring on Jamie Langenbrunner's power-play goal in the second period, then Brett Hull's slap shot at 16:07 of the third. With time slipping away in the overtime, Stars defenseman Darryl Sydor coughed up the puck in the neutral zone, and the Avalanche quickly went to work. Ozolinsh drew Dallas defenders to his side, then zipped a backhand pass across to Drury, who was alone in the circle.

Drury whistled his wrist shot into the near-side corner.

"It was just a great play by Ozo," Drury said. "He made an unbelievable backhand pass right on my tape. I just had to fire it up. I was trying to get as high and up and left as I could."

In the fast-paced overtime, both teams had good chances, but both goalies were spectacular as they turned back shots fired in traffic. Colorado outshot Dallas, 13-8, in the extra period.

Drury fired a one-timer off the faceoff at Belfour, then Peter Forsberg almost crammed the puck past Belfour from the side of the goal. Dallas' Dave Reid fired a wrist shot at Roy, then Mike Modano spun around to send a strong slap shot at Roy.

"He's a great goaltender," Roy said of Belfour. "He's not easy to beat."

The physical game took its toll. Colorado's Milan Hejduk suffered a broken collarbone and is out for the series. Stars defenseman Richard Matvichuk is day-to-day with a strained groin.

"We knew it was going to be a good series," Stars defenseman Derian Hatcher said. "But now, it's going to be a long series."

Both teams could have shortened it. At 12:08 of the overtime, Colorado's Claude Lemieux got called for cross checking Modano. But the Stars failed to take a shot on the power play, despite good chances.

Then, the Avalanche almost scored when Hatcher went off for high sticking Lemieux at 14:36. Stephane Yelle streaked in for a breakaway, but Belfour blocked the backhand shot with his stick pad.

The first two goals marked the first time that Belfour had allowed more than one goal in a period since the second period of Game 4 against St. Louis in the second round—a total of 18

> "We knew it was going to be a good series. But now, it's going to be a long series."
>
> —Stars defenseman Derian Hatcher

The Stars' Derian Hatcher isn't offering a helping hand after decking Colorado's Peter Forsberg during the first period of Game 4 of the Western Conference finals. Hatcher was given two minutes for interference, but the Avalanche didn't score on the power play. (Louis DeLuca, The Dallas Morning News)

> "We got what we came for. It's now a best-of-three, and we have home ice. We have played great in every game in this series. This is what you play for all year, to get to this stage where every player is paying the price."
>
> —Stars coach Ken Hitchcock

periods. But Belfour had no chance on both shots. On the first goal, Sakic sent a long wrist shot at the net while Sydor tried to hold off Theo Fleury at 4:06. Just 48 seconds later, Podein sent a long wrist shot toward the net, and the puck went off defenseman Craig Ludwig's stick and over Belfour's glove on the near side.

The Stars attacked Roy with flurries of shots, including 18 in the second period, their most for one period in the playoffs. On the power play in the second period, Joe Nieuwendyk and Pat Verbeek staked claim in front of Roy while Langenbrunner took a shot from the circle. Roy never saw the puck as it went between his legs at 9:48. With time running out in the third, Nieuwendyk set up the tying goal by getting the puck to Langenbrunner, who got it to Hull. Hull wound up in the right circle, blasting a slap shot that went between Roy's legs.

Despite the Stars' third loss in six playoff overtimes, Hitchcock was satisfied that his team returned to Dallas with a split.

"We got what we came for," Hitchcock said. "It's now a best-of-three, and we have home ice. We have played great in every game in this series. This is what you play for all year, to get to this stage where every player is paying the price."

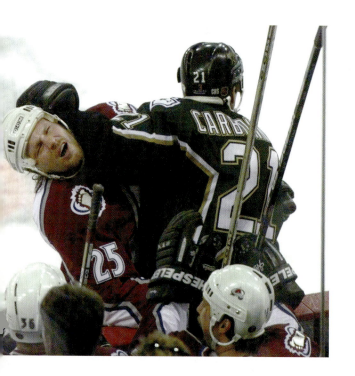

A couple of thirtysomethings tangle during Game 4 of the Western Conference finals in Denver. Dallas' Guy Carbonneau (right) gets pushy with Colorado's Shjon Podein. (Huy Nguyen, The Dallas Morning News)

DALLAS 5, COLORADO 7

May 31, 1999
Keith Gave

PLAYOFFS
WESTERN
CONFERENCE FINALS

# STARS CAN'T WIN SERIES PLAYING AVALANCHE'S GAME

**NBA fans in Dallas who felt cheated out of the hoops playoffs this spring would have loved Sunday's Stars-Avalanche game.**

A concerned Stars bench watches the tide turn in a Game 5 loss to Colorado. (Gary Barber, The Dallas Morning News)

Which pretty much explains why Stars coach Ken Hitchcock didn't care much for it.

His team had more fast breaks (odd-man rushes in hockey parlance) than the Mavericks had all season. Problem is Colorado had even more en route to a wild 7-5 victory that put the Stars on the brink of elimination heading to Denver for Game 6 Tuesday.

"I think we got away from our game a little bit," Dallas captain Derian Hatcher said in what might be the understatement of a promising season suddenly, stunningly slipping away. "It was a run-and-gun game, and I don't know how it happened."

Colorado Avalanche Adam Foote (52) and Dallas Star Blake Sloan (11) battle for position. (AP Photo/Tim Sharp)

The Stars had better figure it out quickly. If they don't, the season is history.

How did it happen? The Stars were uncharacteristically brutal defensively, from the forwards back. And goalie Ed Belfour has had better days in a no-check pick-up game in August.

But Hitchcock preferred to blame the playoff schedule-makers who—because of TV—had the teams facing off less than 38 hours after Friday night's game ended in overtime with a 3-2 Colorado victory in Denver.

"The turnaround was too quick for both teams," he said. "There were some tired people on the ice, and it was pretty obvious who those players were. . . .Some of our slower people today struggled. Really struggled."

Sorry coach, but that sounds like an excuse. Especially for a guy who a few days earlier felt pretty confident about the Stars' depth wearing down an Avalanche club that was relying very heavily on eight forwards and four defensemen. Now who's wearing down?

"The longer this series goes, the better it is for us," Hitchcock has said repeatedly during these Western Conference finals.

Well, here it is—Game 6. And, for the second time, the Stars have squandered home-ice advantage. Now they are forced to win in Denver for the privilege of bringing the series back for a Game 7 crap shoot. So what can we expect?

"I don't know about them, but we need rest," Hitchcock said.

Sorry again, but there's plenty of time to rest in July and August—especially after the parade this city is planning.

Time to suck it up and start playing Dallas Stars hockey again. We've heard a lot about how the team that can impose its will on the other will win this series. Again, that's a Dallas strength. But we saw both sides engaged in a wide-open free-for-all that Colorado loves to play. So do the Stars, of course, but to their credit even they know they can't win playing that way.

"It's tough to go chance-for-chance with that team," said the Stars' Mike Modano, who had two assists but also finished minus-2. "Give that team enough opportunities, and they'll make you pay. Eventually, they did." Modano's solution: "We have to analyze this game and adjust real quick."

Well, analyze this: When the Stars score five goals at home, they usually win by three. Sunday, they allowed seven - more than they allowed in a game all season—on 26 shots and probably as many scoring chances.

That's Colorado's game. That kind of hockey is highly entertaining, but dumb for Dallas to try to play. And deadly. "It's the smart hockey club that's winning games right now," Modano said. "We have to get back to better checking. And that means everybody, not just three or four guys. Every line has to play better one-on-one hockey. "We have to play mistake-free hockey if we're going to come back here tied, 3-3. We need to do whatever it takes to live another day."

In other words, this is no time for excuses, like being too tired. But it's also a great time to see what this Dallas team is made of. If the Stars don't win Tuesday, they won't win the Stanley Cup. Nor would they deserve it.

That said, keep your calendar clear Friday. This series is coming back for Game 7. It's still way too early to turn to the NBA playoffs.

> "It's the smart hockey club that's winning games right now. We have to get back to better checking. And that means everybody, not just three or four guys. Every line has to play better one-on-one hockey."
>
> —Mike Modano

## PLAYOFFS WESTERN CONFERENCE FINALS

**DALLAS 4, COLORADO 1**

June 2, 1999
Bill Nichols

# ROLLING A 7

*Stars rock Avs to force Game 7*

Dallas' Dave Reid attracts a crowd in front of the Avalanche net and can't avoid Colorado goalie Patrick Roy during Game 6 of the Western Conference finals in Denver. (Huy Nguyen, The Dallas Morning News)

**DENVER**—The Stars were down, but after Tuesday's Game 6, they are definitely not out.

Jamie Langenbrunner's two goals led a furious third-period charge that lifted the Stars to a 4-1 victory over Colorado before 16,061 at McNichols Arena. The comeback win tied the Western Conference finals, 3-3, with Game 7 set for Friday at Reunion Arena.

In a game in which the Stars returned to their tight checking style, they had plenty of players who contributed. But none more than Langenbrunner. Langenbrunner, who scored only 12 goals during the regular season, scored his seventh and eighth goals of the playoffs, including the game-winner.

His rebound of Joe Nieuwendyk's shot at 6:49 of the third period broke a 1-1 tie, then Langenbrunner added the security goal on the power play at 17:15. He finished with seven shots, including a breakaway that Patrick Roy stopped.

"You play the game to score goals," Langenbrunner said. "You always dream about scoring goals, when you're in your basement, in the Stanley Cup playoffs."

With the top line of Mike Modano, Brett Hull and Jere Lehtinen struggling to score goals consistently, Dallas' second line of Nieuwendyk, Langenbrunner and Dave Reid has taken control of this

Dallas Stars left winger Jamie Langenbrunner, front, misses this shot, but scored three others in a 4-1 victory over Colorado. (AP/Photo/Bryan Kelsen)

series. Nieuwendyk has nine goals and five game-winners, and Reid has two goals and five assists.

That's why the Stars are going to Game 7, unlike last season, when their offensive limitations kept them from overcoming Detroit in the conference finals.

"Last year, we didn't have two consistent lines," said Reid, who assisted on two goals Tuesday. "You know Mike and Brett and Jere are going to do their thing. It's important to have a second strong push."

It seemed fitting that the Stars, after losing two straight to the Avalanche, would send the series to Dallas by coming from behind. They've done it throughout the playoffs, outscoring opponents, 23-9, in the third period.

But this time, they had no margin for error. Facing elimination, the Stars dominated by playing their style of hockey against a team that had forced them to play a run-and-gun style in Game 5. Thus, the Stars have yet to lose three straight games.

"It was surprisingly loose," Stars wing Mike Keane said of the mood in the dressing room before the game. "We knew if we played the way we can play, we'd win. We have to be a very stubborn team, get the puck in deep and roll four lines."

The Stars did all that. They stuck to the Avalanche with a strong forecheck, played strong positionally to reduce Colorado's odd-man rushes, and were smart defensively.

Dallas outshot Colorado, 40-27, and goaltender Ed Belfour made 26 saves after getting rattled for six goals in Game 5.

> "It was surprisingly loose. We knew if we played the way we can play, we'd win. We have to be a very stubborn team, get the puck in deep and roll four lines."
>
> —Stars wing Mike Keane

"We were a little undisciplined with the puck," Colorado's Theo Fleury said. "We owned the first period. We got the puck in deep, we forechecked them. When they made it 1-1, we tried to press a little bit for the next goal."

With time running out in the first period, Colorado's Adam Foote took a shot from the point, then Claude Lemieux deflected it between Belfour's legs with 35 seconds left in the period.

That score could have sucked the life out of the Stars, but it seemed to incite them.

They scored 1:55 into the second period, when Lehtinen scooped up a rebound and beat Roy high on the glove side. The score stayed that way until 6:49 of the third, when Langenbrunner poked a rebound under Roy's pad.

"We just stayed with it," Langenbrunner said. "We kept coming at them, and when we do that, we get a lot of chances."

Dallas got a big break when Lemieux pushed Belfour down after he had made a save at 16:19. Lemieux's penalty for goaltender interference gave the Stars a power play, setting up Langenbrunner's shot into an empty net after Roy had made a save on Nieuwendyk's shot.

The Stars closed the scoring when Guy Carbonneau got the faceoff back to Richard Matvichuk, who blasted a slap shot past Roy, high on the stick side.

"We just wanted to get our organized game back," Stars coach Ken Hitchcock said. "So the focus was more on positional play. We kept things in control and didn't get running around."

**DALLAS 4, COLORADO 1**

June 5, 1999
Tim Cowlishaw

# NEAT!

### Keane's starry night makes everyone look good

**It was more than just keen, it was unbelievable, really. But it was definitely Keane.**

It was the biggest hockey night Texas has ever known. It was almost without question the biggest sports event involving a local team ever staged in 19-year-old Reunion Arena. And even though the third goal never came, Mike Keane's performance in the Stars' decisive 4-1 victory over the Colorado Avalanche deserved a hat trick.

Keane made golfers of his former Colorado teammates. The Avalanche has not been to the Stanley Cup Finals since he left. This is no coincidence.

Last, but far from least, he delivered the Dallas Stars to hockey's promised land. After an interminable wait—OK, maybe six years isn't exactly forever—the Stars are in the Stanley Cup Finals.

It all starts here Tuesday night against Buffalo, and it's not all because of Keane, but the 185-pound winger came up huge Friday night. He turned what was a very nervous Stars' team (and crowd, it seemed) into a triumphant, exuberant one with second-period goals barely four minutes apart.

That elevated a 1-0 lead to 3-0, stuffing Colorado in a hole that the Stars' suffocating defense turned into a coffin.

"The second goal Keane's first was the big one for us. It turned our nervousness into energy," coach Ken Hitchcock said.

Dallas Stars center Guy Carbonneau, right, rushes to congratulate right wing Mike Keane after scoring a second period goal in Game 7. (AP Photo/Donna McWilliam)

Colorado's Sandis Ozolinsh (8) gets tied up by Dallas' Jamie Langenbrunner (15) and Richard Matvichuk (24) during Game 7 of the Western Conference finals at Reunion Arena. The series finale ended a frustrating post-season for Ozolinsh, who finished with a team-worst minus-5 rating. (Huy Nguyen, The Dallas Morning News)

Dallas' Mike Keane stuffs the puck between Colorado goalie Patrick Roy and defenseman Adam Foote for his second goal of the second period and a 3-0 Stars' lead in the final game of the Western finals, a 4-1 Dallas win. Keane played on Colorado's 1996 Stanley Cup team. (Huy Nguyen, The Dallas Morning News)

It turned the Avalanche into Northwest Division Champs . . . and nothing more.

Hitchcock called the game textbook Stars hockey, and it was. Add up all the shots, missed shots and opponents' blocks, and you can see how dominant Colorado was in the first period. They had 21 total shot attempts to the Stars' eight.

But count just the shots on goal and Colorado's edge was a slim 6-4. Thanks to Jamie Langenbrunner's ninth goal of the playoffs, the Stars had a 1-0 lead despite Colorado having dominated the first 20 minutes.

Once Keane ignited the offense in the second period, the Avalanche slipped away very quietly.

"He is such an emotional player, he lives for this time of year," Hitchcock said of Keane. "His experience going through this, especially with Colorado, he knew the challenges. He was able to pace himself during the season, knowing he would have to blow it out now."

Keane deflects all credit as a goal-scorer. He scored just six during the season but has registered five in the playoffs. His second goal Friday, carrying the puck from inside his own blue line all the way to the net and firing past Patrick Roy, was no grinder's goal.

"I knew Sandis Ozolinsh was behind me, and Adam Foote played the pass all the way. I just carried it in and hoped it wouldn't bounce off my stick," Keane said.

Before long, the towel-waving crowd started up a chant never before heard in Reunion. "We want the Cup. We want the Cup."

This was a game where, well, you didn't have to be there, but if you scalped your tickets, you blew it.

Give Keane credit on a night to remember. And give Bob Gainey credit, too. Keane's former Montreal teammate obtained Keane and Brian Skrudland at the trade deadline a year ago. They weren't the final pieces to the Cup puzzle last year.

A year later, who knows?

"I think Mike Keane's play in this series—you could make a videotape and show it at a clinic," the Stars general manager said. "Tonight, he broke Colorado's back with his second goal."

Keane has won a Stanley Cup in Montreal and another in Colorado. He has two tattoos of the Cup on his ankle, symbols of both.

Maybe he'll have to make a visit to Deep Ellum in two weeks for a third.

"All through the playoffs, somewhere, somehow, someone comes up and makes a big play," said center Mike Modano. "Tonight, it was Keane."

The tattoos serve notice he has had bigger nights. Hockey in the city of Dallas hasn't.

# STANLEY CUP FINALS

**BUFFALO 3, DALLAS 2**

June 9, 1999
Tim Cowlishaw

# SABRES SHOCK STARS IN SERIES OPENER

**A funny thing showed up at the Stanley Cup Finals opener on Tuesday night. And I'm not referring to choppy ice, NHL commissioner Gary Bettman or Stars fans in their seats for the opening face-off.**

I'm talking about something a great game has lacked for five years.

And that's great games. Entertainment.

Four consecutive 4-0 sweeps in the Finals have done nothing to enhance the popularity of a sport that struggles to keep its national TV ratings higher than Buffalo Sabres goalie Dominik Hasek's goals-against average.

This one doesn't have the look of a sweep.

At least, the Stars are praying that's the case.

Buffalo got outshot, 37-24, put the Stars on the power play 10 times and generally looked like a team shaking the dust from a nine-day layoff Tuesday night.

Buffalo also was a 3-2 overtime winner, thanks to Jason Woolley's rip past Stars goalie Ed Belfour 15:30 into the extra period.

"The good thing is we can't get swept now, anyway," Sabres coach Lindy Ruff said. "We just won one for the East."

Buffalo winger Vaclav Varada (left) grimaces after being injured during the third period of Game 1 of the Finals as the Stars' Darryl Sydor skates by. (Louis DeLuca, The Dallas Morning News)

Stars fans whoop it up after Dallas took a 1-0 lead, but they left Reunion Arena dejected following an overtime defeat at the hands of the Sabres. (Randy Eli Grothe, The Dallas Morning News)

Talk about getting caught up in the Stanley Cup Finals. Stars center Guy Carbonneau has his sweater held by the Sabres bench during Game 1 of the Finals at Reunion Arena. (Huy Nguyen, The Dallas Morning News)

The Western Conference's 12-game winning streak in the Finals came to an end Tuesday. The Stars' pursuit of their first Stanley Cup did not, but it's obvious a different Dallas team needs to show up Thursday night for Game 2.

While many were singing the praises of Hasek (and rightly so), Stars center Guy Carbonneau wanted none of that.

"I don't think he was the difference," Carbonneau said. "We were kind of weak at times and didn't play with passion, the passion we had the last two games."

It was probably the Stars' dominance of the Colorado Avalanche in Games 6 and 7 of the Western Conference finals that caused them to be regarded as such solid favorites in this series. At least it's the only reason that comes to mind.

With the Stars having become such a trendy pick to win the Stanley Cup Finals, I spent the better part of Tuesday searching for trends that would suggest Dallas to be anything more than a slightly superior team to the Sabres.

I was still looking midway through the third period Tuesday, when Stu Barnes tied the score at 1-1.

I still hadn't found anything when Wayne Primeau slapped a nifty backhand past Belfour with less than seven minutes to play.

When Jere Lehtinen tied the score with 49 seconds to go in the third period, well, that brought one advantage to mind. Any team with Lehtinen, the Selke Trophy-winning grinder, rates an edge.

I made the personal choice of "Stars in six" based on little more than having picked Dallas at the start of the season and because of the home-ice advantage Dallas has carried through the playoffs. There really isn't that much else that separates these clubs as was evident in Game 1 at Reunion Arena.

Let's look at some of the prevailing theories regarding Dallas' advantages entering the series. There was the thinking that the Stars were more proven, having won the last two Presidents' Trophies as the best regular-season team in the league. But these are the playoffs, and the Sabres are right there with Dallas in the post-season. The last two years, Buffalo is 23-8 in the playoffs. The Stars are 22-13.

This season, Buffalo rolled into the Stanley Cup Finals while losing only three games. Dallas lost five, but the Stars played better teams, right? Isn't that the thinking? Look again. Buffalo's three opponents totaled 291 points during the regular season. Dallas' opponents had 263 points.

And if there was one place in which Dallas definitely lacked an edge, it was simply at the most important position in all of team sports. Hasek showed why he is the Dominator in the first two periods, holding his team in despite almost the entire game having been played in the Stars' offensive zone.

He even made two overtime saves after losing his stick.

The Stars don't need to dwell on Hasek right now. They just need to get mad.

That was Stars coach Ken Hitchcock's biggest concern entering this series. And now we know why.

"If you look at the intricacies of the series, we're not mad at this team yet," Hitchcock had said Tuesday morning. "Buffalo has that built in by being a seventh seed."

In other words, the Sabres have been forced to answer critics and doubters since April, when they swept favored Ottawa. The Stars, knowing or at least believing they just defeated the team most likely to keep them from the Cup, have not worked up a good hate for Buffalo yet.

Anger-management class resumes Thursday night.

**DALLAS 4, BUFFALO 2**

June 11, 1999
Bill Nichols

# STARS STRIKE BACK IN GAME 2

*The Stars got mad. They also got even.*

After getting outhit in Game 1 of the Stanley Cup Finals, Dallas pounded out a 4-2 victory over the Buffalo Sabres in Game 2 on Thursday that tied the best-of-seven series, 1-1.

Brett Hull got the game winner with a slap shot past Dominik Hasek at 17:10 of the third period. Derian Hatcher added an empty-net goal with 26 seconds left before 17,001 towel-waving fans at Reunion Arena.

That ended a furious contest that saw Stars center Brian Skrudland charge Hasek in the first period, Mike Modano trip Hasek at the end of the first and left Buffalo coach Lindy Ruff intimating that he would like those plays reviewed by league officials.

The hard-hitting contest also left Modano with a sprained wrist that has the Stars' top player listed as day-to-day entering Game 3.

The Stars were well aware of the game's significance after having lost Game 1 at home. Game 2 has great historical significance, too. The team that has won Game 2 has won 26 of the past 28 Stanley Cups, including every series in the last 10 years.

Stars players had read comments from the Sabres saying they were laughing during Game 1 because they were so confident they would win.

After being outhit in Game 1, 60-44, the Stars struck back with a 48-38 advantage in hits. And their aggressive play created much better scoring chances because there was more traffic in front of Hasek.

Brett Hull (right) celebrates with Shawn Chambers (left) and Tony Hrkac after giving the Stars a 3-2 lead over Buffalo with fewer than three minutes to play in the third period of Game 2 of the Finals. While the goal was Hull's seventh of the post-season, it was his first game winner after recording 11 of them during the season. (Erich Schlegel, The Dallas Morning News)

Buffalo defenseman Alexei Zhitnik (44) was the Sabres' leader in hits through the Finals. During the third period of Game 2 at Reunion Arena, his target was Stars defenseman Richard Matvichuk. (Erich Schlegel, The Dallas Morning News)

Even all-star goalies sometimes need someone to fill in while they tend to other business. During Game 2 of the Finals, the Sabres' net was left in the capable hands of defenseman Jay McKee (74) after Dominik Hasek had fallen. (Louis DeLuca, The Dallas Morning News)

"I heard they were laughing and smiling during the last game," said Skrudland, who was penalized for charging Hasek in the first period. "We've got three more wins before our team can start smiling. Both teams are fighting for the Stanley Cup. We wanted to send a message."

Hull's shot did just that. His blast whistled off the near-side post, just inside Hasek's left shoulder. It was his first game winner in the playoffs.

The Stars had signed Hull last July to score big goals in big games. But before Thursday's game, Dallas was only 1-5 in playoff games in which Hull had scored. But after Shawn Chambers and Tony Hrkac got control, with Hrkac passing to Hull in the face-off circle, Hull let loose with a rocket that Hasek never had a chance to save.

"It was a great play by Chambers and Hrkac," Hull said. "I just teed it up."

The Stars were intent on initiating the physical action, rattling the boards for 42 hits in the first two periods. After Michael Peca's power-play goal gave Buffalo the lead at 7:27 of the second, the Stars climbed back with Jamie Langenbrunner's goal with 1:34 left in the second.

The teams traded hard hits, with Dallas doing most of the instigating, and the bad blood boiled over at the end of the first period.

On the last shift, Modano tripped Hasek. Then Langenbrunner skated up to Hasek for a heated discussion. That brought the wrath of Buffalo defenseman Alexei Zhitnik, who cross-checked Langenbrunner. As Zhitnik and Langenbrunner squared off, Dallas veteran Joe Nieuwendyk traded punches with Brian Holzinger for only the third fight of Nieuwendyk's career. And Stars captain Derian Hatcher rumbled with Richard Smehlik.

When the dust cleared, Nieuwendyk and Holzinger were given five-minute fighting penalties, and Modano, Hatcher, Zhitnik and Smehlik got two-minute penalties.

"It was definitely a cheap shot by Modano," Ruff said. "He went through the crease and slew-footed Hasek. There are always ways to combat it. I don't even want to talk about that."

The scrum seemed inevitable because of the tight-checking pace. In the first period, the Stars outhit the Sabres, 30-11,

Stars winger Blake Sloan slides into Sabres goalie Dominik Hasek during Game 2 of the Stanley Cup Finals at Reunion Arena. Sloan, a late-season pickup from the Houston Aeros of the International Hockey League, earned regular ice time throughout the playoffs because of his grit and energy. (Louis DeLuca, The Dallas Morning News)

but took only five shots. Dallas didn't get its sixth shot until nine minutes into the second. Buffalo landed a damaging blow when Darryl Sydor took a penalty for hooking at 5:41. With 14 seconds left in the power play, Jason Woolley passed from the point to Peca, who was standing alone beside the goal. Peca, waving his stick to attract a pass, easily beat Ed Belfour with a one-timer at 7:27.

"We caught them on a change and a regroup," Peca said. "I snuck around the net, and Jason Woolley made a great play."

But the Stars increased the offensive pressure. Nieuwendyk zipped the puck to Richard Matvichuk at the point. As Matvichuk took his slap shot, Langenbrunner, fighting two defenders in the slot, stuck out his stick to redirect the puck over Hasek's right shoulder.

Craig Ludwig then gave Dallas the lead at 4:25 of the third with his first goal in 102 playoff games, knocking in a slap shot off the face-off, which Skrudland won.

The Stars had the lead for only 1:11.

## STANLEY CUP FINALS

**DALLAS 2, BUFFALO 1**

June 13, 1999
Bill Nichols

# NIEUWENDYK TAKES CHARGE

**BUFFALO, N.Y.**—Mike Modano played with a severely injured wrist. Brett Hull left after his third shift with a groin injury. And Benoit Hogue and Grant Marshall have yet to play in the Stanley Cup Finals.

Buffalo's Miroslav Satan and Dallas' Derian Hatcher mix it up. (Louis DeLuca, The Dallas Morning News )

So, it seems fitting that a player who missed last season's playoffs because of an injury held the Stars together … again … in Game 3 of the Stanley Cup Finals against the Buffalo Sabres.

Joe Nieuwendyk continued his magical playoff run, scoring both Dallas goals Saturday night in a 2-1 victory before 18,595 at Marine Midland Arena.

Nieuwendyk's 10th and 11th goals of the post-season were his biggest. They allowed Dallas to come back from a 1-0 deficit and hand the Sabres their first loss in nine home playoff games this year.

With Nieuwendyk taking charge on offense and Dallas shutting down Buffalo's strong power play, the Stars regained control of the best-of-seven series, two games to one. Dallas limited the Sabres to 12 shots, tying a Finals record for fewest shots allowed.

The Stars are two wins from their first Stanley Cup in franchise history, with home-ice advantage back on their side.

And after a knee injury suffered in the first post-season game knocked him out of last year's playoffs, Nieuwendyk has established himself as the

The travels of the goalies—and their eligibility to legally receive hits from skaters—became an issue during the Finals. Dallas' Ed Belfour (right) takes a whack at Buffalo's Richard Smehlik after going back behind his net to play the puck. (Louis DeLuca, The Dallas Morning News)

Veteran Stars center Guy Carbonneau prepares for another faceoff during Game 3 of the Finals in Buffalo. Dallas dominated this critical area of the game throughout the playoffs, and many Stars players credited tips from Carbonneau for their faceoff success. (Huy Nguyen, The Dallas Morning News)

leading candidate for the Conn Smythe Trophy as the playoffs' most valuable player.

His 11 goals lead all players, and his sixth game-winner tied the NHL record held by Colorado's Joe Sakic.

"He's played like he's on a mission," Stars coach Ken Hitchcock said. "He just doesn't want the season to end."

Nieuwendyk, Jamie Langenbrunner and Dave Reid have been Dallas' strongest line. They have combined for 23 goals. With Modano sporting a soft cast and Hull … leaving the ice after a first-period hit by Buffalo defenseman Alexei Zhitnik, Nieuwendyk's line again took charge.

Nieuwendyk evened the score at 15:33 of the second period when he took a pass from Reid, fired a shot that Dominik Hasek blocked, then backhanded the rebound past Hasek on the far side as Erik Rasmussen knocked him down.

On the game-winner at 9:35, Langenbrunner took control in the corner, spun away from defenseman Richard Smehlik and zipped a pass through traffic to Nieuwendyk in front. Nieuwendyk quickly worked the puck to his forehand and whistled a shot into the upper near-side corner.

"It was difficult last year not being a part of it," Nieuwendyk said. "Especially at this point, when you realize what it takes to go through this playoff run. So I'm just thrilled to death to be healthy and playing and doing what I can to help this team win."

Nieuwendyk had help from a suffocating defense that blocked more shots (19) than Stars goalie Ed Belfour saved (12) and penalty killing units that allowed only five shots on Buffalo's eight power plays.

By shutting down the power play, the Stars eliminated the Sabres' biggest strength. The Sabres entered the game 3-for-8 with a man advantage. But they got nowhere with the power play, including a five-on-three in the first period.

"It's tough to explain," Buffalo coach Lindy Ruff said. "They did a number on us. We weren't very creative, and we didn't get many shots through. A lot of the credit goes to them."

Modano's status was in doubt until the opening faceoff. But he came out for the first shift and played his normal roles on the power play and penalty kill. His injury was hardly noticeable. He took five shots, blocked three shots and sprang teammates with good passes. He also got three penalties.

Modano lost his right winger, Hull, early in the first period. On his third shift, Hull was hit hard at center ice by Buffalo's Zhitnik. Hull, who scored the winning goal in Game 2, did not return because of what was listed as a groin injury.

Having another key player go down hardly mattered to the Stars. Tony Hrkac moved up to left wing on the top line. Jere Lehtinen, who regularly plays left wing on the Modano line, moved over to the right. "We lost Brett, and it took us 15 minutes to tell he wasn't out there," Guy Carbonneau said. "But don't tell him that."

The Stars kept the Sabres on the perimeter. And when they weren't blocking shots, they were clearing bodies from in front of Belfour. It was a textbook road game for Dallas, which patiently stuck to its physical defensive game, forced mistakes, then pounced on offensive chances.

"They gave us a good lesson there," Ruff said. "They suffocated us."

The Stars knew they faced a tough chore because of all the talk of payback for their harassment of Hasek in Game 2. But it was Buffalo that looked tense as the Stars limited the Sabres to 12 shots.

"That's Dallas Stars defense right there," Stars defenseman Richard Matvichuk said. "We knew we had to weather the storm the first 10 minutes because they were going to be pumped up."

The Sabres scored first, at 7:51 of the second period, when center Stu Barnes zipped the puck into an almost-empty net after Belfour had gone down for a shot. Despite committing five penalties in the first period and three in the second, the Stars never panicked. They seemed to feed off their success on the penalty kill.

"I really think that was the difference for us," Hitchcock said. "That gave us so much energy. There was just so much confidence for us to be able to kill those."

After Nieuwendyk tied the score with 4:27 left in the second period, Dallas dominated the third. They outshot the Sabres, 8-3. Now they have two days off to heal and contemplate Game 4, also in Buffalo.

"This is a great position to be in, to let them think about it for two days," Modano said. "This can really get the momentum going."

BUFFALO 2, DALLAS 1

June 16, 1999
Keith Gave

STANLEY CUP FINALS

# DRAMATIC HASEK COMES UP WITH BRILLIANT PERFORMANCE

**BUFFALO, N.Y.**—The world's finest goaltender is a lousy actor, and he would do wonders for his reputation if he just stuck to stopping pucks.

Buffalo's Dominik Hasek might have led an inspired effort in a 2-1 victory Tuesday night over Dallas in Game 4 of the Stanley Cup Finals that evened the teams' best-of-seven series at two games each. But he soiled an otherwise brilliant, 30-save performance with a series of smarmy dives and pratfalls that don't even fool the referees anymore.

How many Hart and Vezina trophies does he have to win to convince him that we appreciate his good work? Isn't he secure atop the pyramid of goaltenders after that phenomenal, gold-medal-winning performance in the 1998 Olympics?

Why, then, must he continue to make himself the center of attention with all the silly theatrics? Like charging out of the crease to mug Stars

The boards behind the net are not a place for the meek. Dallas' Pat Verbeek gets sandwiched between Buffalo goalie Dominik Hasek and defenseman Richard Smehlik during the third period of Game 4 of the Stanley Cup Finals at Marine Midland Arena. (Louis DeLuca, The Dallas Morning News)

Stars defenseman Craig Ludwig can only glance back at goalie Ed Belfour after a giveaway by Ludwig led to the Sabres' go-ahead goal during Game 4 of the Stanley Cup Finals in Buffalo. The Sabres' Dixon Ward took the suddenly loose puck and gave Buffalo a 2-1 lead at 7:37 of the second period, and the score stood up. (Huy Nguyen, The Dallas Morning News)

The Stars' Joe Nieuwendyk (25) fends off Buffalo's Michael Peca (far left) and Jason Woolley to try to keep control of the puck during the first period of Game 4 of the Stanley Cup Finals in Buffalo. (Huy Nguyen, The Dallas Morning News)

defenseman Derian Hatcher after the horn sounded to end the first period. Like ranging out of his net, as he did a few seconds earlier to play the puck, then taking a spectacular dive when he made incidental contact with Joe Nieuwendyk.

If Stars goalie Ed Belfour did that, the hockey press would be all over him for caving in to the stress. Hasek does it repeatedly, and we wink at it saying, "Ah, that's just Dom."

Truth is, interference-running, stick-tossing, referee-baiting tactics are shameful. And they detract from Hasek's otherwise wonderful game. The guy even tripped coming back to the bench after taking a post-game twirl after being named the game's No. 1 star. Should we inquire if his tender groin is OK for Game 5?

Sadly, Hasek has plenty of company on both sides in the diving department, and it's time for the referees to call somebody's bluff. Call the unsportsmanlike penalty that's on the books for such blatant attempts to draw penalties. The NHL finally has a great Stanley Cup Finals, and it's turning into World Cup soccer with all the players rolling around faking falls.

But there is no denying, as much as Stars coach Ken Hitchcock tried in his post-game news conference, that the series is tied because Hasek, the Sabres' one legitimate superstar, was their best player when they needed him most. Hasek was a lot better than "OK," as Hitchcock described him; just don't get the Stars coach started on the other silly elements to Hasek's game.

The save alone that Hasek made with 7:40 remaining on Dave Reid was worth the price of admission at Marine Midland Arena. Reid scooted behind the net from left to right and tried to flip the puck high, as instructed, over Hasek, who was prone on the ice. But Hasek managed to get a glove up and make the save.

Hasek also deserves credit for daring his teammates to play with more grit and guts, saying "the whole team should be more aggressive ... Go after them," he said.

And, so the Sabres did, pressuring the Stars' defense into making two critical mistakes that led to both goals. Now, instead of the Stars giving themselves a chance to win the Stanley Cup in Game 5, it's a best-of-three series. And though the Stars have home-ice advantage, the Sabres are coming hard with a ton of confidence forged by Hasek's challenge that he backed up by going after Hatcher, the Stars' biggest, toughest player.

"He said it all right there," Buffalo coach Lindy Ruff said. "He just figured that if this team was going to get going physically and emotionally, then he was the leader for us. He just said, 'Bring it on.'"

Ruff doesn't even mind seeing his best player getting involved physically, though to accuse Hasek of fisticuffs would be giving him far too much credit. He wouldn't dare drop his glove.

"He's got a black belt," Ruff said. "He'll be all right."

Hasek certainly would be if he borrowed a page from teammate Dixon Ward's book. Ward scored the go-ahead goal early in the second period on a wicked wrist shot through a screen past Belfour. It would stand as the game winner.

But Ward barely celebrated the goal, neither raising his stick in celebration nor sharing a group hug with his teammates. Rather, he skated directly to his bench to prepare for the next shift in what he described as the most important game of his life.

"Trying to be less flamboyant," Ward explained. "Just trying to do my job."

Hopefully, his goaltender was paying attention.

> "He just figured that if this team was going to get going physically and emotionally, then he was the leader for us. He just said, 'Bring it on.'"
>
> —Buffalo coach Lindy Ruff

# STANLEY CUP FINALS

DALLAS 2, BUFFALO 0

June 18, 1999
Keith Gave

# MODANO ANSWERS THE CALL

**Ken Hitchcock dialed 9-1-1, and Mike Modano picked up the phone.**

"What kind of player are you going to be?" the Stars coach asked his best player on the eve of their most important game of the season.

"I told him I would be very involved in every aspect of the game," Modano said.

Promises are made to be broken, but, if anything, that one might have been a little understated. Modano ... broken wrist and all ... wasn't merely better Thursday night in a 2-0 victory over Buffalo that gave his team a 3-2 lead in this marvelous Stanley Cup Finals series.

Modano assisted on both goals. And when he didn't have the puck, he was a back-checking, penalty-killing maniac, logging more ice time than any forward in the game. He even found time to double shift and center the "Gimp Line," with wingers Brett Hull (who has been listed with a groin injury) and Benoit Hogue (a knee injury).

And Hitchcock, who has been lighting these fires under Modano since he became coach midway through the 1995-96 season, deserves a big assist for inspiring this kind of play. The best coaches get the best efforts from their best players in the most important games. This was one of those special moments for player, coach, teammates and fans. At least the 17,001 at Reunion Arena seemed to appreciate it.

"Going into the game tonight, I thought [Buffalo] had an X-factor [in

Pat Verbeek celebrates a goal scored by teammate Darryl Sydor during the second period of the Stars' Game 5 victory at Reunion Arena. Verbeek scored the insurance goal that gave Dallas a two-goal cushion at 15:21 of the third period. (Huy Nguyen, The Dallas Morning News)

Linesman Jay Sharrers (center) tries to break up this difference of opinion between Sabres forward Miroslav Satan (left) and Stars defenseman Derian Hatcher during the first period of Game 5. (Huy Nguyen, The Dallas Morning News)

Buffalo goalie Dominik Hasek receives an unscheduled visit from Dallas' Jamie Langenbrunner during the second period of Game 5 of the Finals at Reunion Arena. (Huy Nguyen, The Dallas Morning News)

Before Buffalo's Wayne Primeau (left) can't get to the puck, Stars goalie Ed Belfour pounces on it to force a faceoff during the third period of Game 5 at Reunion Arena. Belfour recorded his seventh career playoff shutout, stopping 23 Sabres shots. (Louis DeLuca, The Dallas Morning News)

all-star goalie Dominik Hasek], and I thought Modano was our X-factor," Hitchcock said. "For us to win this series, Mike had to be a player of significance, whether he scored a point or not in the game. And he made a big step in that direction today."

Indeed, Modano continues to disprove critics who have questioned his heart since he was the first NHL draft pick overall in 1988.

That was him flying across the blue line and kicking up snow as he stopped on a dime at the top of the face-off circle. That was him, pausing and faking a defender before he threw the puck across the ice, a perfect tape-to-tape pass to Darryl Sydor. A perfect shot and a 1-0 lead, just what Modano ordered the day before with a suggestion that sounded an awful lot like a challenge for his team to consider winning a game like that for a change.

So, as you would expect, that was Modano defending that slim lead with redoubtable passion until he started the play that gave his team some much-needed breathing room with a second goal with 4:39 left in the game. He's the guy who beat Sabres defenseman Alexei Zhitnik in a battle for the puck along the boards and kicked it up ice. Seconds later, Pat Verbeek was in alone and flipped the puck past Hasek with a nifty backhander.

The Stars are at their best offensively when they can deliver a one-two punch with the top two lines centered by Modano and Joe Nieuwendyk. In a 2-1 loss in Game 4, they were missing that, with Hull out with his injury and Modano admitting his head wasn't completely in it because of his painful left wrist.

With Nieuwendyk contained and frustrated to the point that he dropped his gloves to scuffle for the second time in this series, Modano emerged as the offensive force. His two assists gave him a share of the team playoff scoring lead with Nieuwendyk. Both have 21 points, and that's a career-high for Modano.

Clearly, Modano's left hand was feeling better, and it showed when he was able to put a little mustard on the three shots that he recorded. But what he is showing the world in these Finals is that his game is so much more rounded. And what he is showing his coach and teammates is that they can depend on him when he's needed most.

That means playing defense, winning face-offs (he won 18 of 26), killing penalties and getting involved in the scrums … all part of his game along with the two plays that directly led to the game's only goals.

"It's a great responsibility. But when you're able to do that, you feel better about your game, personally," he said. "And you feel better when you leave the rink."

When Modano left Reunion after Thursday's game, he had every reason in the world to feel very proud of himself and his game. Because he knows not only that his team is within one victory of the greatest prize in the game, but also how very difficult it is to achieve.

One more win, and he can change his phone number and get a break from his coach.

June 19, 1999
Gerry Fraley

# BENOIT HOGUE

**Benoit Hogue put a price on the Stanley Cup.**

His career.

Hogue, defying medical predictions, returned to the Stars' lineup on Thursday night for Game 5 of the Stanley Cup Finals against the Buffalo Sabres at Reunion Arena. Hogue took a huge gamble to have a chance at putting his name on the Cup.

"I've never been this close," Hogue said. "I might never be this close again. I have to play. This is the Stanley Cup."

The risk involves Hogue's left knee.

Hogue tore the knee's anterior cruciate ligament during the second game of the Western Conference finals against Colorado on May 24. Orthopedists said Hogue needed surgery and a six-month rehabilitation period.

Hogue put off the surgery in hopes of returning for the Finals. That put his knee and his future in jeopardy.

By playing, Hogue exposes the knee to more injury.

"Anybody is at risk out there, even if they don't have a knee injury," said Hogue, who wore a protective brace on the knee. "I don't think I'm at risk any more than anybody else."

Dallas Stars coach Ken Hitchcock his team from the bench in the first period against the Detroit Red Wings in Game 2 of the Western Conference Finals in Dallas, Tuesday, May 26, 1999. (AP Photo/Bill Waugh)

In late season action against Phoenix, Coyotes goaltender Nikolai Khabibulin, Dallas Stars forward Benoit Hogue keeps his eye on the puck. (AP Photo/Mike Fiala)

Hogue has delayed the surgery for three weeks. That is significant, because Hogue will become a free agent after this season.

Hogue cannot avoid the surgery and the recovery period. That means Hogue probably will not be able to play until December, at the earliest. That will decrease his value on the free-agent market.

There is not a great demand for a 32-year-old winger who will miss the first two months of the regular season.

"If this was a contracted player, a player that had a future that was locked in and guaranteed, then there is no doubt he would be on crutches and rehab," Stars coach Ken Hitchcock said. "This is a player who has no contract. At the end of the season, he's got nothing except his goodwill and his play. He wanted to back that up.

"That's the thing I admire more than anything. He's willing to risk that ... to play in the Stanley Cup. That should be admired."

Hogue played on the Joe Nieuwendyk line in the first two rounds of the playoffs. Hogue had only two assists, but he figured in the line's overall success with his ability to move bodies and create space.

Hitchcock decided not to return Hogue to that line. Dave Reid took his spot and had played well.

Hogue also played on the penalty-killing units. In the 12 playoff games through Hogue's injury, the Stars killed 44 of 49 penalties.

"If he can get somewhere close to the player he was before getting hurt, we've got a lot of options," Hitchcock said.

This is Hogue's first appearance in the Finals. The hockey gods owed him this.

Hogue joined the Stars in the midst of the horrid 1995-96 season, in which Dallas finished 26-42-14 and missed the playoffs. He signed with Tampa Bay as a free agent for this season and suffered through 62 games with the league's worst team.

"I want to be here for the good times after going through some of the bad times," Hogue said.

That is why Hogue refused to give up on this chance. It is a priceless opportunity.

> "If this was a contracted player, a player that had a future that was locked in and guaranteed, then there is no doubt he would be on crutches and rehab. This is a player who has no contract. At the end of the season, he's got nothing except his goodwill and his play. He wanted to back that up."
>
> —Stars coach Ken Hitchcock

## STANLEY CUP FINALS

June 19, 1999
Bill Nichols

# LORD STANLEY IN STARS' SIGHTS

Stars coach Ken Hitchcock makes it clear to linesman Kevin Collins that he isn't happy about a call during the third period of Game Two of the Finals at Reunion Arena. (Huy Nguyen, The Dallas Morning News)

**BUFFALO, N.Y.**—The Stars are one victory away from winning the Stanley Cup. But the Buffalo Sabres will not go quietly.

Trailing the best-of-seven series three games to two entering Saturday's Game 6, the Sabres on Friday accused the Stars of being a dirty team with players who use their sticks like hatchets.

The Stars responded by saying that hockey is a rough sport, and they will do whatever it takes to win.

And the verbal sparring between coaches Ken Hitchcock of Dallas and Lindy Ruff of Buffalo, who shouted at each other after Game 5 at Dallas' Reunion Arena, continued in separate news conferences.

Ruff accused Hitchcock's team of being goons. Hitchcock then blasted Ruff for trying to create controversy that could influence the way on-ice officials call the game. Hitchcock also said that Ruff substituted a physical player, Rhett Warrener, on the last face-off of Game 5 so that he could go after Stars defenseman Derian Hatcher.

Dallas' Mike Modano (9) gets tangled up with Sabres' Alexei Zhitnik during the third period of Game 3 of the Finals in Buffalo. Despite suffering a cracked wrist in Game Two, Modano put in a full night's ice time in Game Three. (Louis DeLuca, The Dallas Morning News)

Dallas' Joe Nieuwendyk collides with Buffalo goalie Dominik Hasek and doesn't mind a bit. That's because he just put the puck past Hasek during the second period of Game Three of the Finals to tie the score at 1-1. (Louis DeLuca, The Dallas Morning News)

"As vicious as that team is with their sticks, [Buffalo assistant coach] Mike Ramsey's comment was, 'On the offense, they go with their soft sticks and on defense they swing by the bench and pick up their hatchets,'" Ruff said. "It is true. You watch Pat Verbeek play, he turns his stick over all the time. It is a two-handed swing. It is vicious …

"Watching the tape, you probably see between five and 10 really good two-handers, baseball swings where guys are turning their sticks over … Our guys are not going to lay down. I still think, in our building [Saturday] night, the physical play is going to be something that is very evident."

When hard-hitting Game 5 ended in a scrum, Hatcher was pulled off of Warrener. Warrener was helped off the ice, his ankle broken. Ruff said he though Hatcher sucker-punched Warrener. Ruff all but promised payback for Warrener's injury, even mentioning players who would be targets. He said that his team would not go after Hatcher, who is 6-5.

"We'd go after after [Guy] Carbonneau, [Joe] Nieuwendyk or [Mike] Modano," Ruff said. "We're not going to be in a situation like David and Goliath."

Carbonneau, Modano and Pat Verbeek rolled their eyes as Ruff's quote was paraphrased to them by a reporter at their news conference.

"I don't think we try to hurt players, but we'll do anything to win the game," Carbonneau said. "If they don't like it, that's too bad. We have only one thing on our mind, and that's winning the Stanley Cup."

In Buffalo's Eastern Conference finals series against the Toronto Maple Leafs, Ruff accused Toronto coach Pat Quinn of sending out enforcers to take runs during the final shifts while Buffalo was leading Games 2 and 3, calling Quinn "classless."

Hitchcock said that Ruff was doing the same thing as Quinn on the last face-off in Game 5. He said that was the subject of his post-game argument with Ruff as the two were leaving their respective benches.

"In my opinion, a skilled player was taken off the ice and a tough player was put on the ice," Hitchcock said. "The face-off puck dropped, and Warrener went after Hatcher, and that is fine. "But Lindy is the same guy that was complaining at Pat Quinn for doing the same thing in the last series. So, don't go and play the almighty when we both know, as coaches, what the message was. Lindy and I know why Warrener was out there at the end of the game, and I was very upset about that."

Ruff said he put Warrener out there to protect his players from Hatcher. "Hatcher is by no means a clean player, and Rhett had his back turned to him and was getting pushed from behind … and he is not going to back down. He wasn't out there to fight, but he was out there to look after [other players]."

Buffalo captain Michael Peca said that the Stars "are probably the dirtiest team I've ever faced. Maybe part of being as experienced as they are is knowing how to hide the two-handed slashes."

Verbeek, mentioned by Ruff as a dirty player, clenched his jaw when asked to respond.

"I play to win, and I try to play within the rules," Verbeek said. "I don't play to have a nice time out there. I play to make sure that you know that I am on the ice, and I don't want to be an easy guy to play against. I have played that way my whole career, and that's what has got me here, and it's what will keep me here."

Hitchcock said Buffalo's comments were a ploy to get officials on the Sabres' side. He said the same thing about the Sabres' comments before the first game about how Dallas players cheat on face-offs.

"When you start barking like this … obviously, you are hoping that the referees read the papers. Why don't we just let the players decide the outcome, because I am sure our players can talk about some of the dirty deeds that happen."

And considering the verbal jousting, there should be plenty to talk about after Game 6.

### DALLAS 2, BUFFALO 1

June 20, 1999
Bill Nichols

# TRIPLE OVERTIME TRIUMPH!

**BUFFALO, N.Y.**—Some kept pushing on blown-out knees, novocaine deadening the pain. Others revived themselves in the dressing room between periods with IV tubes that squeezed saline into their bloodstreams.

Six players, including five with damaged medial collateral ligaments in their knees, took injections to stay on the ice with injuries that otherwise would have kept them off.

The Stars paid the price. And they got the Stanley Cup in return.

The pain inherited from 23 playoff games, including eight overtimes, was masked by their smiles at having achieved a lifelong dream. After beating the Buffalo Sabres, 2-1, in triple overtime early Sunday morning, the Stars laughed, hugged and cried, smoked cigars and drank champagne.

"We had the IVs going, the saline bags going, and everybody's shooting that up and trying to find some energy, trying to find something extra," said Stars center Mike Modano, who played with a broken bone in his

Dallas' Brett Hull (left) raises his arms in celebration after getting the puck past Buffalo's Dominik Hasek at 14:51 of the third overtime to end Game 6 at Buffalo and give the Stars their first Stanley Cup. The game was the longest in NHL history that determined a Cup champion. (Louis DeLuca, The Dallas Morning News)

The Dallas bench erupts moments after Brett Hull's goal clinches the Stanley Cup. From left are Mike Keane, Richard Matvichuk, Blake Sloan, Brian Skrudland and Joe Nieuwendyk. (Michael Mulvey, The Dallas Morning News)

left wrist. "Everybody was just dying."

When Brett Hull scored the winning goal at 14:51 of the sixth period, it seemed a fitting end to the Stars' quest. He was the key free agent signed after last season's loss in the Western Conference finals, brought in for big-game goals.

But Hull wasn't even supposed to be on the ice.

The Sabres argued afterward that Hull's skate was in Dominik Hasek's goal crease. And replays clearly showed it was. But league officials said that Hull had control of the puck from the time he first took a shot at Hasek, then kicked the rebound onto his stick, which made the goal legal. A player in control of the puck can have his skate in the crease, even before the puck, said Bryan Lewis, NHL director of officiating.

"There's no controversy there," said Joe Nieuwendyk, who was awarded the Conn Smythe winner as most valuable player of the playoffs. "The puck went in, and we got the trophy.

Brett Hull does what his father, Bobby, did with the Chicago Blackhawks following the '61 Finals—hold aloft the oldest trophy in North American sports. Hull was going to be benched for the remainder of Game 6 because of multiple injuries and was only on the ice at the time he scored the series winner because other players were unavailable for various reasons. (Louis DeLuca, The Dallas Morning News)

Stars center Guy Carbonneau sips some champagne from the Stanley Cup during the celebration in the visitors' dressing room in Buffalo after Game 6. Carbonneau had previously won the Stanley Cup as a Montreal Canadien in 1986 and '93. (Louis DeLuca, The Dallas Morning News)

That's all I know.

"To win the Cup and the Conn Smythe … I never would have dreamt it after double knee surgery over the summer. It's just been an unbelievable run, an unbelievable feeling."

Hull playing hurt epitomized the character of his team, which methodically grinded its way to its second consecutive Presidents' Trophy and then over Edmonton, St. Louis, Colorado and Buffalo in the playoffs without losing more than two consecutive games. Key players went down, and they were replaced without the team ever missing a beat.

The Stars opened the scoring in Game 6 on Jere Lehtinen's goal at 8:09 of the first period on a shot that snuck in a small opening between Hasek's right pad and the right goalpost. But they seemed in slow motion as Buffalo rattled them with 82 hits and tied the score on Stu Barnes' goal in the second period.

Belfour—as he did the entire season and especially the playoffs—kept Dallas in the game, by making 53 saves.

By the third overtime, the stubborn Stars had worn down their younger opposition.

"The first two periods, when the game was really revved up, we were struggling to keep up," Stars coach Ken Hitchcock said. "In the third overtime, it looked like we had lots of gas. Because the game had slowed down, we were stickhandling in the phone booth and everything."

Hull, a future Hall of Famer whose resume lacked only a Stanley Cup, had blown out a knee on an open-ice hit from Alexei Zhitnik in Game 3. The Stars kept it undercover by saying he hurt a groin. The other injuries never were mentioned because the players kept playing.

"I thought I was finished, but I said, 'What the hell? There's only two games left, let's figure out a way to do it,' " Hull said. "We taped it up, we numbed it up, we put a brace on it. For the Stanley Cup, I think you risk everything."

The Stars had eight veterans who had won 10 previous Cups, including Mike Keane, who now has one with three franchises.

But they also had veterans such as Verbeek, Dave Reid, Tony Hrkac and Hull, and core players such as Modano, captain Derian Hatcher, Sergei Zubov, Darryl Sydor, Jamie Langenbrunner, Richard Matvichuk and Lehtinen, who never had hoisted hockey's ultimate prize.

"We fought through a lot of stuff, last year and this year," Hatcher said. "We faced a lot of adversity in the playoffs this year, and this team always responded."

While the Stars had plenty of talented players, depth was the key. They blended experience and youth, and each knew his role.

In the end, they were battered and bruised, but they had come too far to fall short.

"Sometimes destiny is there, and you just have to march into it," general manager Bob Gainey said. "And I think we had the right makeup, and the right spirit, to do it."

## STANLEY CUP FINALS

June 20, 1999
Tim Cowlishaw

# CHAMPIONS!

Goalie Ed Belfour is mobbed by his teammates after his stellar performance in Game 6. (Louis DeLuca, The Dallas Morning News)

**There was a distant look in the eyes of the doctor. A disbelieving look, too.**

Stars orthopedist Dan Cooper had just walked out of the training room after the club's Game 5 victory at Reunion Arena on Thursday night, June 17.

"You won't believe what's going on in there," he said, shaking his head. "When this is over, I'll tell you about it."

And the following Saturday night—make that Sunday morning—it was over and the Stars were champions of the National Hockey League.

Given the talent on their roster, that's not so amazing. Given the health of their roster, it's flabbergasting.

This team won a Stanley Cup with heart when it should have been buried by wounded knees.

Stars coach Ken Hitchcock told part of the story, probably the biggest part, in his post-game news conference after the triple-overtime clincher when the subject turned to Brett Hull. The game-winning goal in the Stanley Cup was supplied by a player who, in the words of captain Derian Hatcher, "never should have been on the ice."

In keeping with hockey's time-honored custom of lying about injuries, Hitchcock had called Hull's injury a groin pull. Actually, that wasn't a total fabrication because he did have a torn groin.

And Hitchcock had hinted before Game 5 that Hull had something worse. In truth, he had a Grade 3 tear of the medial collateral ligament in his left knee.

Team owner Tom Hicks is among the celebrants after the Stars' triple-overtime victory over Buffalo in Game 6 of the Stanley Cup Finals. (Louis DeLuca, The Dallas Morning News)

Champagne spray is the order of the day in the Stars' locker room soon after Dallas defeated Buffalo in Game 6 of the Stanley Cup Finals. (Louis DeLuca, The Dallas Morning News)

"I think when the dust settles, the story on Brett Hull is going to be an incredible story," Hitchcock said. "We hid a lot of things and what this man did to get on the ice, what we had to do between periods to get him back on the ice. He might not be rehabbed enough to start the season."

Hitchcock didn't even want to play him in overtime. But rookie Blake Sloan was having back problems and veteran Benoit Hogue, also playing with a torn MCL, was having skate problems. So, back Hull skated into the fray.

"I think I now realize what the sacrifice is to win the Stanley Cup," said Hull, who never got past the second round in 10 seasons with St. Louis. "I am looking forward to not having to practice for awhile."

Cooper, who also works with the Dallas Cowboys, never has been more surprised to see an injured athlete perform.

"It takes tremendous heart and soul to do what he did," said Cooper.

In all, the Stars had five players with torn medial collateral ligaments by the end of the series—all still playing.

Cooper gave injections to Hull, Hogue, Pat Verbeek, Darryl Sydor and Guy Carbonneau in order to freeze their knees and get them on the ice for Game 6. Also, he gave another injection to Mike Modano because of the broken wrist that he suffered in Game 2.

"Guys were dehydrating in overtime," Cooper said. "I gave Guy Carbonneau two liters of IV after one overtime period and another two liters to Modano. Shawn Chambers had to have his knee drained to keep going.

"To tell you the truth, I felt like a flight surgeon trying to keep paratroopers ready for battle."

Hull's courage was already high on Modano's list, but he discovered newfound respect for him in Game 6.

"Brett could barely move out there," Modano said. "We just told him to get to the front of the net, and somehow we'd get the puck to him."

Somehow, despite an overwhelming number of injuries that were kept in the dark, the Stars persevered. And consider for a moment the man who led them. Center Joe Nieuwendyk picked up the Conn Smythe Trophy as the playoffs' most valuable player. He scored 11 goals, a figure that included six game-winners. It was a year ago that Nieuwendyk was knocked out of the playoffs in the first-round opener against San Jose with a major knee injury.

"I don't believe anyone in the history of sports has come back to be a playoff MVP the year after having major ACL reconstruction," Cooper said. "And Joe had two of them. I saw him crying in the off-season. I know what he went through."

We knew the Stars were old. We didn't know they were crippled.

They could become the first world champions in history to gain full handicap parking privileges in the process.

"It was so tough last year not being a part of the playoffs, going down early," said Nieuwendyk. "I was able to win the Cup at 22 [in Calgary], and I was a bit naive. Ten years later, you realize what a battle it is to get here—all the injuries, all the adversity.

"It's just one battle after another, and it makes it all worthwhile in the end. It's been a great ride for us."

Wounded and scarred along the way, the Stars rose above it all to capture a championship and a city's hearts.

Maybe some purple hearts, too.

> "It's just one battle after another, and it makes it all worthwhile in the end. It's been a great ride for us."
>
> —Joe Nieuwendyk

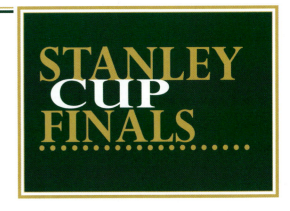

June 22, 1999
Keith Gave

# CELEBRATION!

**BUFFALO, N.Y.**—Bob Gainey could have stood there amid the champagne spray in the Stanley Cup championship dressing room and said, I told you so. But he didn't. Truth is, he was second-guessing himself along the trail.

Ed Belfour couldn't peel off his sweat-soaked goaltender's equipment fast enough before screaming, *I told you so* to all his second-guessers. But he didn't. His actions spoke for themselves, but he did have a few things on his mind.

Kyle Verbeek, at age 10, is a bit too young for second-guessing. All he knows for sure is that this might be the best Father's Day he'll ever share with his dad, Pat.

These were some of the sweet moments enveloped by chaos early Sunday morning in the visitors' dressing room at Marine Midland Arena, where moments earlier the Stars had just claimed their first NHL title with a 2-1 victory over the Buffalo Sabres well into the third overtime of Game 6 of the Stanley Cup Finals.

As you would expect, the winning goal that video replays suggested might not have been entirely kosher wasn't much of a topic of discussion while a bunch of guys sprayed bubbly all over the room. That was someone else's headache. The Stars would have theirs the next day, unless some chose to stickhandle around their hangovers by just not going to sleep.

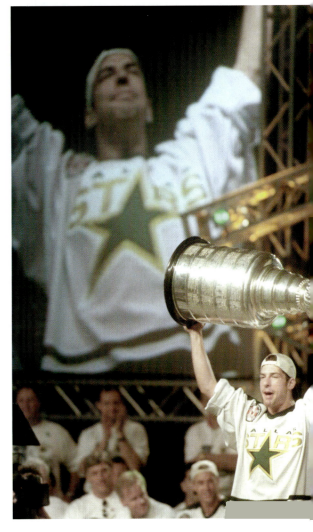

It's Darryl Sydor's turn to take a spin around the Reunion Arena stage with the Stanley Cup—his image also projected on a video screen in the background—during the post-parade rally on June 21. (Michael Mulvey, The Dallas Morning News)

Mike Keane holds the Stanley Cup high during the June 21 parade in Dallas. (Huy Nguyen, The Dallas Morning News)

Fans enjoy the Stanley Cup parade in downtown Dallas, two days after the Stars defeated Buffalo in the sixth game of the Stanley Cup Finals. (Huy Nguyen, The Dallas Morning News)

The valiant Sabres had a pretty good argument that game and league officials botched the call on the winning goal, when Brett Hull's skate was clearly in the crease when he scored.

But that wasn't the league's only questionable call Saturday. Ballots for the Conn Smythe Trophy that goes to the most valuable player of the playoffs overall were collected with more than 10 minutes remaining in regulation. The game, as it turns out, was not even half complete.

Had the vote been tallied after the game, Belfour might have completed his charge from behind to overtake Joe Nieuwendyk, who graciously conceded that Belfour was at least as worthy a candidate.

Not that it mattered. Belfour got what he came for—a Stanley Cup title that many said he could never deliver because he's so emotionally volatile. "Over and over, they said I couldn't do it," Belfour said. "Now, finally, people can shut up as far as I'm concerned. They said all that stuff, how I couldn't do this, couldn't do that. Well, I love proving people wrong … "I just feel an incredible inner satisfaction. It's been a lifetime of hard work and dedication. This is a dream come true—finally."

And finally, those steely blue eyes began to soften. Belfour's voice quivered with emotion as he continued: "It's just such a great feeling to be on this team with these guys. We're brothers for life now. We're bonded together forever. I'll never forget this day as long as I live. It's the happiest day of my life."

Gainey, the architect of this team, hasn't had many happier ones himself on the professional side of his ledger. And here's a guy who as a player won five Stanley Cup titles as a player with the Montreal Canadiens.

When other Western Conference powers like Detroit and Colorado made major moves in late March to rev up their rosters for the playoffs, Gainey boldly stood pat. But while he loved his team's chemistry, he frequently wondered if it was deep enough for a long playoff run.

"There were times that I really thought we should have had another player or two," he confessed. "But the group found a way to buy enough time to get the injured guys back and get

Star fans cheer as their heroes and the Stanley Cup make their way through downtown Dallas during the June 21 parade. (Andy Scott, The Dallas Morning News)

through it. And in the end, we played with the goalie, the six defensemen and the 12 forwards we started out with."

What especially pleased Gainey, though, was how his team dealt with the tremendous expectations that began Day 1 of training camp in Vail, Colorado, last September. Anything short of a championship parade would have been a disappointment. Fair or not, that is a tremendous burden for a team to live with for nine months. But the Stars delivered.

"They were always there, and we weren't shying away from anything," Gainey said of the lofty goals set for this team. "If anything, we attacked them head on."